THE ART OF chocolate

techniques & recipes for simply spectacular desserts & confections

BY ELAINE GONZÁLEZ

photographs by Frankie Frankeny

dedication

FOR PEPE,

WHO LOVINGLY PAVED MY WAY

Library of Congress Cataloging-in-Publication Data:

González, Elaine.
    The art of chocolate: techniques and recipes for simply
spectacular desserts and confections/by Elaine González;
photographs by Frankie Frankeny.
        p.   cm.
    Includes bibliographical references and index.
    ISBN 0-8118-1811-x (pbk.)
    1. Cookery (Chocolate) 2. Chocolate. 3. Desserts.
    4. Confectionery. I. Title
TX767.C5G63 1998
641.6'374—dc21   98-11491
                                                          CIP

Printed in Hong Kong.

Chocolate provided by Peter's Chocolate, Division of Nestlé U.S.A.
Food styling by Wesley Martin and Elaine González
Design and Typesetting by
    Juliette Robbins for Danielseed Design

The photographer wishes to thank Anne Galperin, Bill LeBlond,
    Leslie Jonath and Sarah Putman at Chronicle Books for their
    belief in me, and Wesley Martin for his grace on such a
    detailed project. Also Alison Richman, who helped with the
    little things so I could concentrate on the bigger ones. And
    thanks to Philip Le Four at Made in France for his help at the
    beginning of the project.

Distributed in Canada by Raincoast Books
8680 Cambie Street
Vancouver, British Columbia V6P 6M9

10 9 8 7 6 5 4 3 2

Chronicle Books
85 Second Street
San Francisco, California 94105

www.chroniclebooks.com

the art of chocolate

CHRONICLE BOOKS
San Francisco

acknowledgments

The process of writing a book can be compared to giving birth—to a behemoth hippopotamus! Mine was a real labor of love, for me as well as my family. From its very conception (no pun intended), my husband, Pepe, and our children, Jay, Carla, and Lisa, were incredibly patient and kind—especially during those difficult times when the words did not come easily and I really needed their support. I can't thank them enough for everything they did to help me.

I am also immensely grateful to Malcolm Blue, a true chocolate visionary, who recognized my potential before anyone else did and then gently guided me in the right direction. Thank you, Malcolm, for being my angel, and my champion, my mentor, and my friend.

Peter's Chocolate, the chocolate and confections division of Nestlé U.S.A., also played an enormous role in the development of my career. I am deeply indebted to Richard Prezzano and all of the district managers for their steadfast support over the years and for their generous contributions to this project. I am particularly grateful to Randy Hofberger, Nestlé's technical manager and resident chocolate wizard, who is always an invaluable source for technical help when I need it.

My extended family, friends, and colleagues have given me unconditional support and assistance throughout the writing of this book. I especially want to thank my mother, Mary García, and my sister, Louise Harrison, as well as Maria Battaglia, Maria Kijac, Pam Vieau, Ruth Siegel, Sue Cortesi, Kathleen Jurkowski, and Ken and Dixie Stetson. I am also grateful to my literary agent, Susan Ginsburg, for believing in me, and Bill LeBlond, Sarah Putman, and Carolyn Miller at Chronicle Books for breathing life into my words.

contents

contents

❧ Chocolate Fondue Birdbath with Chocolate Bird, page 124.

introduction

Working with chocolate is a magical experience. Transforming a pool of liquid chocolate into spectacular desserts and confections has an aura of mystery about it that most people find fascinating. As magical a phenomenon as it may seem, however, with a little know-how the process of creating beautiful things from chocolate can be quite simple.

My approach to working with chocolate is relaxed and low-key, relying more on common sense and ingenuity than fancy techniques and artistic ability. You may find this statement surprising, given chocolate's reputation for being demanding and unpredictable, but before long, you will know it to be true. When handled correctly, chocolate is a forgiving and responsive medium.

The methods I have developed through years of working with chocolate are technically sound and easy to understand, yet never simplistic. I don't ignore the key issues regarding the proper handling of chocolate. Instead, I identify chocolate's idiosyncrasies and deal with them honestly—in simple terms, with simple solutions.

Whether you are a beginner, an accomplished candy maker, or a long-time baking enthusiast, you will find this book filled with enough information and creative stimulation to satisfy your curiosity and feed your artistic spirit. With clear, easy-to-understand instructions, I'll show you how to go beyond simple molding and basic decorating to create masterpieces in chocolate.

My techniques for working and playing with chocolate will enable you to mold free-form shapes, pipe intricate designs, make picture-perfect confections, create stylized chocolate containers, and assemble spectacular centerpieces. Before long, you'll be rolling, curling, twisting, coaxing, and nudging chocolate like a master chocolatier.

Since aspiring chocolatiers also need a repertoire of high-quality recipes for cakes and chocolate-laced desserts, I've included a chapter of basic cakes, fillings, frostings, and sauces, plus another chapter showing how to combine these elements with chocolate decorations to make simply spectacular cakes and desserts.

My main purpose in writing this book is to share what I've learned about chocolate. I want to reveal secrets, clarify misconceptions, and explain things clearly, in simple terms. More than anything, I want my words to inspire you to enjoy working with chocolate and to encourage you to make your own spectacular chocolate creations.

BASIC EQUIPMENT

❧ Top row, left to right: cake pan, glass laboratory thermometer, rubber spatulas, metal spatulas, craft knife

❧ Middle Row, left to right: grid-type wire cake rack, instant-read thermometer, nested stainless-steel mixing bowls, microwave container

❧ Front row: Acetate strips

SPECIALTY TOOLS

❧ Wall, left to right: dipping fork, 10-inch pastry bag, 3- and 6-inch wall scrapers, 100-count ice cream scoop, artists' brushes

❧ Table, left to right: square notched adhesive spreader, pastry bag tips #1, 10, 12, and large size #1A, 2-piece plastic coupler, small cookie cutters, scriber tool, assorted kitchen cabinet molds, chocolate chipper, gold luster dust

1

ingredients and tools

ingredients

CHOCOLATE AND CONFECTIONERY COATING

Chocolate is made from beans that grow inside the pods of cacao trees, which flourish in hot, rainy climates within 20 degrees of the equator. Cocoa beans, as they are known in the United States, don't develop their distinctive chocolate color, flavor, and aroma until they have been fermented, dried, and carefully roasted to precise temperatures. The roasted beans are then shelled and cracked into small pieces called nibs. The nibs are then ground, producing a thick, semifluid mixture called chocolate liquor, the primary ingredient in all forms of chocolate (except white chocolate).

Making chocolate is an art as well as a science. Chocolate manufacturers guard their formulas under lock and key, never divulging them. Also kept secret are the roasting temperatures, the time given to "conching" (a mixing, heating, and rubbing action that produces fine-flavored, smooth, and mellow chocolate), and the exact proportions used in their formulations—which explains why no two manufacturers' chocolates taste the same.

All brands of chocolate fall into one of four categories: unsweetened, sweetened dark, milk chocolate, and white chocolate, with cocoa powder in its own separate category. One or more of these kinds of chocolate are available in the baking and candy sections of most supermarkets, in many specialty foods stores, and through mail-order catalogs. (There are also specialty chocolates and confectionery coating; see below.)

Once you determine the *type* of chocolate you need, select a corresponding brand that fits your budget. As you gain experience working with chocolate, you'll learn to discern one kind from another so that you can make intelligent choices based on your own needs and personal taste preferences (see page 5).

Unsweetened Chocolate

Unsweetened chocolate is chocolate liquor. Also known as bitter, baking, or cooking chocolate, it is pure chocolate: ground roasted cocoa beans with no other added ingredients. Because cocoa beans are nearly equal parts cocoa butter and cocoa solids, unsweetened chocolate imparts a deep, rich chocolate flavor to anything you make with it.

Unsweetened chocolate is combined with sugar to make American-style cakes, brownies, frostings, and fudge. It is also the basic ingredient used in the manufacture of all other types of chocolate (except white chocolate). By law, all products labeled "chocolate" (except white chocolate) must contain unsweetened chocolate (sometimes listed on the label as cocoa solids and cocoa butter, or chocolate liquor).

For home cooks, unsweetened chocolate is sold in 8-ounce packages containing individually wrapped 1-ounce pieces. Popular supermarket brands include Baker's Unsweetened Baking Chocolate Squares, Ghirardelli Unsweetened Chocolate, Hershey's Premium Unsweetened Baking Chocolate, and Nestlé Toll House Unsweetened Baking Bar.

Sweetened Dark Chocolate

The chocolates in this category, variously named extra bittersweet, bittersweet, semisweet, and sweet chocolate, are the ones you will use most frequently for baking, candy making, and fancy decorative work. They contain varying amounts of chocolate liquor and sugar, extra cocoa butter, vanilla or vanillin, and lecithin; butterfat is an optional ingredient. These chocolates are interchangeable in most recipes, but as their differences can slightly alter the flavor, texture, and appearance of the finished product, always try to use the chocolate specified in the recipe.

Bittersweet bars, which contain the most chocolate liquor (at least 50 percent), cocoa butter, and not more than 12 percent milk solids, often have a deeper chocolate flavor than those labeled "semisweet," and are apt to be less sweet. The amount of sugar that they contain is not regulated, however, so what is bittersweet to one manufacturer may be semisweet to another. Popular choices available in retail stores include Dröste Bittersweet Pastilles, Ghirardelli Bittersweet, Chocolat Lindt Excellence, Chocolat Lindt Rod Lindtfils, Tobler Tradition, and Valrhona Le Noir Gastronomie and Equatoriale.

Semisweet chocolate must contain at least 35 percent chocolate liquor and not more than 12 percent milk solids. Choices include Baker's Semi-Sweet Baking Chocolate Squares, Dove Dark Chocolate, Ghirardelli Semi-Sweet Baking Chocolate, Guittard Real Semisweet, Hershey's Premium Semi-Sweet Baking Bar, Hershey's Special Dark Sweet Chocolate, Nestlé Toll House Semi-Sweet Baking Bar, Perugina Dark Chocolate, and Sarotti Extra Semisweet. To find the one you like best, sample several brands.

"Sweet" dark chocolates are the sweetest ones in this category and have the mildest taste, because they contain the least amount of chocolate liquor (15 to 35 percent) and no more than 12 percent milk solids. Popular choices include Baker's German's Brand Sweet Chocolate Bar, Ghirardelli Sweet Dark Baking Chocolate, and Hershey's Dark-Mildly Sweet Bar.

Milk Chocolate

Milk chocolate contains less chocolate liquor (10 percent minimum) than the dark chocolates, more sugar, and at least 3.39 percent butterfat and 12 percent milk solids, which is why it is considerably lighter in color and less intensely chocolate flavored than the others. Its high sugar content and heat-sensitive milk solids make it a poor choice for baking but an excellent choice for candy making.

These popular brands can be found in the candy sections of most supermarkets: Cadbury Dairy Milk, Chocolat Lindt Swiss Milk, Dove Milk Chocolate, Ghirardelli Milk Baking Chocolate, Hershey's Milk Chocolate Bar, Nestlé Milk Chocolate Giant Bar, and Perugina Milk Chocolate.

White Chocolate

White chocolate contains a minimum 20 percent cocoa butter, 14 percent milk solids and a maximum 55 percent sucrose (sugar), but no chocolate liquor, which is why it is ivory, not brown. The cocoa butter gives it a subtle milk chocolate flavor and a smooth, creamy mouth feel. It is used in cheesecakes, light-textured cakes, confections, frostings, and decorations for its delicate chocolate flavor and its pale color.

Don't confuse white chocolate with white confectionery coating, which contains a vegetable fat other than cocoa butter (see page 4). Always look for the words *cocoa butter* on the wrapper. White chocolate is also distinguishable by its ivory color, the telltale sign of cocoa butter's presence.

Supermarket brands include Baker's Premium White Chocolate Baking Squares, Dröste White Pastilles, Ghirardelli Classic White Baking Confection, Lindt Swiss White Tablette Blanche, and Perugina White Chocolate Bar.

Cocoa Powder

Unsweetened cocoa powder is pulverized, partially defatted chocolate liquor. Two types are available in supermarkets: natural (nonalkalized) and Dutched or Dutch-process (alkalized), named in honor of the Dutch chemist who invented it, Coenraad van Houten.

Natural cocoa is light in color and somewhat acidic, with a strong chocolate flavor. In baking, use natural cocoa in recipes that call for baking soda (because it is an alkali). Combining natural cocoa (an acid) with an alkali such as baking soda creates a leavening action that allows the batter to rise during baking.

Dutch-process cocoa has been processed with alkali to neutralize its natural acidity, so it is darker (sometimes with a reddish cast), milder in taste, and less acidic than the nonalkalized kind, even though its color suggests that *it* is the stronger-flavored of the two. Use Dutch-process cocoa in recipes that call for baking powder as the primary leavener. If alkalized cocoa is combined with baking soda (another alkali) in a cake recipe, it will create an overabundance of alkali in the batter. As a result, the batter will not rise properly, and the cake will have a "soapy" taste. In recipes where no leavening is required, you can use either one.

Until recently, almost all alkalized cocoa was imported from Europe, but American brands are now available as well. Do not confuse either of these cocoa products with cocoa powder mixes, which contain dry milk powder, sugar, and flavorings.

Natural (nonalkalized) cocoa powders include Ghirardelli Premium Unsweetened Cocoa, Hershey's Cocoa, and Nestlé Toll House Cocoa.

Dröste Cocoa, Van Houton Cacao (cocoa), and Hershey's European Style "Dutched" (alkalized) Cocoa are available in most supermarkets. Bensdorf, DeZaan, Lindt, Pernigotti, Valrhona, Van Leer, and Merckens Dutch-process cocoas are sold in specialty foods stores and through mail-order catalogs (see page 150).

Specialty Chocolates

Chocolate Chips: Chocolate chips have come a long way since Ruth Wakefield, the owner of the Toll House Inn, mixed some broken bits ("morsels") of a Nestlé semisweet chocolate bar into a batch of her favorite cookie dough and created the most famous cookie in the world, the Toll House cookie.

Today, chocolate chips come in many sizes and flavors. They are formulated to withstand normal oven heat and to hold their shape in cookies, muffins, and other baked desserts without melting, even though the cocoa butter is fully melted. When forced to melt, the chocolate is thick, muddy, and difficult to use, because it contains less cocoa butter (about 26 to 29 percent) than the average bar chocolates. For that reason, chocolate chips should not be used in recipes that call for melted chocolate—despite any directions to the contrary. Instead, substitute an equal amount of bar chocolate.

I admit to being loyal to Nestlé Toll House Morsels (Semisweet, Mini, Mint, and Milk), the originator of this type of chocolate. Other supermarket brands include Baker's Real Chocolate Chips; Ghirardelli's Semi-Sweet, Milk, and Double Chocolate Chips; Guittard Real Semisweet and Milk Chips; and Hershey's Milk, Semi-Sweet, and Raspberry-Flavored Semi-Sweet Chocolate Chips.

Couverture Chocolate: Couverture, which means "coating" or "covering," is a term used for cocoa butter–rich chocolates of the highest quality. These chocolates, which contain high percentages of chocolate liquor (sometimes more than 70 percent) as well as cocoa butter (at least 32 to 39 percent), are very fluid when melted and have an appealing mellow flavor.

During their manufacture, couvertures undergo an intense mixing, heating, and rubbing process known as conching, which smooths out the roughness of the sugar particles and removes the harsh flavor notes, giving them a creamy mouth feel and a mellow flavor. Confectioners regularly use couvertures to enrobe pieces of candy in a thin coating of chocolate, to mold thin hollow shells, and to make all kinds of spectacular chocolate creations.

Today, famous couvertures like Cacao Barry, Callebaut, Peter's Chocolate, and Valrhona, which once were available only to professionals, are now sold in upscale gourmet shops and through mail-order catalogs. The closest things to couvertures in most supermarkets are the imported chocolate candy bars. The word *couverture* probably won't appear on the wrapper, but the price will often distinguish them from bars of lesser quality. Popular retail brands include Lindt, Succard, and Tobler. See "Buying Chocolate" (page 4) for more information on other brands.

Gianduja: This European favorite (pronounced john-DU-ya) is a creamy blend of milk or dark chocolate and roasted hazelnut or almond paste. It can be used as a flavoring ingredient or as a substitute for milk or dark chocolate in baking and confectionery recipes. At room temperature, it is soft enough to roll into balls or cut into squares for serving as individual candies, but it is too soft to use for molding.

Supermarkets sell two brands of chocolate that resemble gianduja: Dröste Praline and Sarotti Nougat. See "Buying Chocolate" (below) for other brands of gianduja sold in bulk quantities.

Confectionery Coating

Confectionery coatings, which contain a vegetable fat other than cocoa butter, have become very popular with home cooks and confectioners in recent years because they are so versatile and easy to use, even in warm weather. These chocolate lookalikes contain cocoa powder, vanilla, fruit or peanut flavorings, sugar, milk solids, and lecithin, in a vegetable-oil base (usually palm kernel oil) that does not require tempering (see page 20). Though they resemble chocolate in appearance and usage, confectionery coatings have a weaker chocolate flavor and aroma, melt at a higher temperature, and cost less than most brands of real chocolate. Many leave a waxy residue in the mouth, which is caused by the melting qualities of the fats they contain—not by the presence of paraffin (which is not an ingredient). Never combine confectionery coating with chocolate, because the fats are incompatible. Doing so will cause a discoloration to appear on the surface of the chocolate (see page 5).

Confectionery coatings come in a variety of shapes, colors, and flavors. Since they do not contain cocoa butter or significant amounts of chocolate liquor, they cannot be called chocolate, and are instead identified as confectionery coating, compound coating, pastel coating, summer coating, or chocolate-flavored coating.

These coatings, which are sold in wafers, chips, and rectangular shapes, are readily available in cake and candy supply shops and in crafts stores. To distinguish them from real chocolate, check the ingredients listing on the package for the presence of palm kernel oil or another non–cocoa butter fat.

If you are timid about working artistically with chocolate, I encourage you to experiment with these coatings before attempting to use real chocolate. Brands include Nestlé Icecap Caps, Ambrosia Diskin Confectionery Coating, Guittard Pastel Ribbons and A'-Peels, Merckens Rainbow Coatings, Van Leer "Snaps Line," Wilbur Cocoa and Flavored Drops, and Wilton Candy Melts.

Buying and Storing Chocolate and Confectionery Coating

Buying in Bulk: Once you gain some experience, you will probably want to purchase chocolate in bulk form, usually in 10-pound slabs (sometimes broken up into smaller amounts), from mail-order catalogs and specialty foods stores. Bulk chocolates include the very best couvertures, which are not available in smaller bars. Not only is the quality of most bulk chocolate superior to anything that is available in most supermarkets, but it is also less expensive per pound. Buying chocolate in bulk is one of the best investments you can make when you are learning to work with chocolate.

My personal favorites are Chocolat d'Or (semisweet), Alpine (milk chocolate), Burgundy (semisweet), Broc (milk chocolate), and Snowcap (white chocolate), all made by Peter's Chocolate, a division of Nestlé U.S.A. Other brands of bulk chocolates include Belcolade, Blommer, Cacao Barry, Callebaut, Carma, El Rey, Felchlin, Ghirardelli, Guittard, Hawaiian Vintage, Lindt, Merckens, Scharffen Berger, Schokinag, Valrhona, Van Leer, Wilbur, and World's Finest Chocolate's Cook's Gold. Popular brands of gianduja include Carma, Callebaut, and Valrhona. See page 150 for mail-order sources.

Storing Chocolate and Confectionery Coating: Ideally, chocolate and confectionery coating should be stored at 60° to 70° F, in an odor-free place away from heat and direct sunlight, and with a humidity no higher than 50 percent. If the temperature fluctuates too much, the cocoa butter may soften and rise, causing a gray discoloration (bloom) to appear on the chocolate. This is a superficial flaw that will disappear when the chocolate is melted. White chocolate is particularly susceptible to strong light and will turn rancid if exposed to it for even a few hours. Though harmless, this detracts from the flavor of the chocolate.

There is no reason to refrigerate or freeze chocolate unless you live in a hot climate with no air-conditioning. If you must, refrigerate or freeze the chocolate in an airtight container, and do not remove it until it is brought to room temperature or completely thawed. Condensation will form on the surface of exposed cold chocolate brought to room temperature, and the moisture will prevent it from melting smoothly.

Under optimum conditions, dark chocolate will last at least 1 year, milk chocolate 10 months, white chocolate 8 months, and confectionery coating about 10 months.

Choosing the Best Chocolate: Not all chocolates are created equal. You owe it to yourself to consider these qualities and physical conditions when you shop for chocolate:

Select chocolate that has a glossy, unblemished surface. Superficial blemishes on a piece of chocolate do not necessarily indicate that the chocolate is bad or old, but they may be a sign that it has deteriorated to some degree.

Chocolate in good condition will snap cleanly when you break it; otherwise, it will bend or crumble.

Select chocolate that smells chocolaty. If it doesn't smell chocolaty, it probably won't taste very chocolaty either. Stale chocolate often smells bland. Chocolate that is stored near any odor will absorb it quickly, like a sponge. Never buy chocolate that is shelved near tea, coffee, fertilizer, or anything else aromatic.

Judge a piece of chocolate by the way it melts in your mouth. Does it feel sandy, or smooth? A velvety mouth feel is generally preferred—though it often comes with an expensive price tag.

As the chocolate melts, does it taste sweet, bitter, burnt, rancid, vanillalike, or simply delicious? If you like how it tastes, your opinion is as valid as anybody else's.

How fluid is it when it melts? Unfortunately, when you shop for chocolate, you will probably not see any measure of a bar's viscosity (see page 149) on the wrapper, since the percentage of cocoa butter that it contains is rarely given. Generally, the more expensive the bar of chocolate, the more cocoa butter it is likely to contain, and the more fluid the melt. At a supermarket, the bars most likely to melt fluidly will be located in the candy section.

American vs. European Chocolates: There is a distinct difference in taste and texture between European and American chocolates. Europeans favor a smoother texture and a stronger, more bitter taste than most Americans, though the lines are less clearly drawn today than they were ten years ago. The mild flavor and harsh texture that identified American chocolate in the past are no longer entirely representative of the preference today. The influx of imported chocolates opened eyes and raised standards and expectations. Today's best American chocolate is competitive with imported brands from all over the world.

I began using American chocolate more than twenty years ago. Since then, I have had the opportunity to work with nearly every brand of domestic as well as imported chocolate. While there is much to praise about many of the European brands of chocolate, I use American chocolate with excellent results.

FLAVORINGS

Alcohol-Based Flavorings

Chocolate tastes better when it is combined with another flavor. Chocolate and vanilla, for example, have been linked since precolonial times in Mexico, when they were used to prepare intoxicating drinks for the nobility and ritualistic offerings to the gods. Today, manufacturers all over the world still use pure vanilla extract (derived from vanilla pods, the fruit of a vine belonging to the orchid family, *Vanilla planifolia*) or vanillin (an artificial form of vanilla) to flavor chocolate, because they know that it tastes flat without it.

There are many other alcohol-based flavorings that you can add to chocolate to enhance or accentuate its flavor. Just remember to add the flavorings to chocolate *mixtures*, not to pure melted chocolate, lest the alcohol cause the melted chocolate to seize, or tighten into a hard ball. Orange, lemon, almond, coffee, and other extracts are available in the baking section of most supermarkets and in many specialty foods stores and mail-order catalogs.

You can also flavor chocolate candy recipes with your favorite aperitifs, liqueurs, and spirits. My choices often include amaretto (sweet and bitter-flavored almond), brandy, Calvados (apple brandy), Chambord (black raspberry), Cognac, Cointreau (orange), crème de cacao (chocolate), crème de cassis (black currant), framboise (raspberry), Frangelico (hazelnut), Grand Marnier (orange and Cognac), Kahlúa (coffee), kirschwasser (black cherry), dark rum, and whiskey.

Oil-Based Flavorings

Oil-based flavorings can be added directly to melted chocolate to enhance its flavor without affecting its texture. Some oil flavorings, like mint, are potent and should be used sparingly. A strongly flavored piece of mint candy placed in a boxed assortment will permeate the rest, causing all of them to taste like mint in a very short time.

You'll find a variety of oil-based flavorings in specialty foods stores, cake decorating and candy supply shops, and behind the drug counter in many pharmacies, where they are used to flavor medicine. Popular flavors include orange, lemon, cherry, peppermint, spearmint, wintergreen, cinnamon, and raspberry.

It's fun experimenting with different flavor combinations, but it's best to seek a balance between sweet and bitter and/or tart. My favorite flavor combinations with chocolate are apricot, coffee, raspberry, orange, and hazelnut.

NUTS

Candy makers use nuts in, on, and around all kinds of chocolate candies. The most commonly used nuts are almonds, Brazil nuts, cashews, candied chestnuts, coconut, hazelnuts (filberts), macadamias, peanuts, pecans, pistachios, and walnuts. They can be used whole, sliced, slivered, chopped, or ground, as an ingredient in recipes, dipped whole or in clusters, or as a decoration. Salted nuts are rarely used in commercial candy recipes because they become rancid quickly, but it's okay to use them at home if you know that the candy will be eaten in a short time. I like to combine lightly salted nuts with sweet milk and white chocolates.

Store most nuts in airtight containers in the freezer for up to 1 year (rather than at room temperature, where they become rancid quickly). Walnuts, peanuts, and all salted nuts have a shorter shelf life; they can be frozen for up to 10 months.

Toasting Nuts: Toasting nuts brings out their flavor. Spread whole almonds and hazelnuts on a baking sheet in a preheated 325°F oven for about 8 to 12 minutes, or until they're lightly browned and aromatic, turning them once or twice. Oily nuts like pecans and walnuts should be toasted in a preheated 300°F oven for 5 to 6 minutes, or until aromatic but not browned. (In some instances, I prefer to leave pecans raw.) Sliced or slivered nuts will be toasted in about 6 to 8 minutes.

Toasting Coconut: Toast coconut in a preheated 350°F oven for 6 to 8 minutes, stirring frequently to prevent it from burning.

Skinning Hazelnuts, Almonds, and Pistachios: Hazelnuts, almonds, and pistachios taste better if their thin outer skin is removed before using. All can be purchased with or without their skin (blanched), though blanched hazelnuts are harder to find. To remove almond and pistachio skins by hand, soak the nuts in a saucepan filled with hot water (about 195°F) for about 3 or 4 minutes, drain them, and spritz with cold water to remove some of the heat. The skins will peel off easily if you rub or pinch them between your fingers. To remove most of the skin from hazelnuts, toast them first, then wrap them in a thick, coarse cloth; let them steam for 1 minute, and rub them vigorously inside the cloth.

tools

You don't need a lot of fancy equipment to work with chocolate. If you cook or bake on a regular basis, you probably already have most of what you need on hand. As you gain experience, you can add other items. Almost everything you will need is available in hardware stores, cookware and cake decorating shops, office and art supply stores, and through mail-order catalogs (see page 150).

BASIC EQUIPMENT

Cake Pans and Baking Sheets: I recommend using heavy-duty, straight-sided aluminum pans for baking cakes and molding chocolate baskets and boxes with matching lids. It is important to have duplicates of most sizes, since batters are often divided and baked in two pans. Eventually, you will want to have a separate set of shiny, scratch-free cake pans for molding chocolate boxes and baskets. Having multiple baking sheets is convenient for baking as well as for forming individual chocolate candies, rolling out chocolate clay, and many other purposes. I prefer rimless baking sheets for most nonbaking purposes. They enable me to spread and deposit chocolate exactly where I want it without any obstructions. Inverted sided baking pans lined with waxed paper and secured with tape may be substituted. These are the pans you will need for the recipes and techniques found in this book:

> Two 6-by-2-inch straight-sided round pans
> Two 8-by-2-inch straight-sided round pans
> One 8-by-3-inch round pan
> Three 9-by-2-inch round pans
> One 9-by-3-inch round springform pan
> One 9-by-2-inch heart-shaped pan
> One 10-inch pie pan
> Three 13-by-17-inch rimless baking sheets,
>   or three 12-by-18-by-1-inch sided baking sheets
> One 12-by-15-by-1-inch jelly roll pan

Craft Knife: A craft knife with a thin, sharp, retractable blade known as a "goat's-foot blade" is another invaluable tool. Some people use them to trim wallpaper, open boxes, or cut linoleum, but I use them to score and cut pieces of chocolate. These knives are inexpensive and easy to find in hardware stores and crafts shops.

Double Boiler: Double boilers provide gentle, indirect heat for melting chocolate. A conventional double boiler is composed of two stacked saucepans, the lower one holding an inch or so of hot, but not simmering, water and the other the chocolate to be melted. I actually prefer using a stainless steel bowl set over a saucepan, because it's easier to stir chocolate in a curved bowl than in a straight-sided saucepan. If you like that idea, be sure to select a bowl that fits snugly over the pan to prevent accidental water spills and/or the escape of steam, which could cause the chocolate to thicken into a hard lump.

Electric Mixer: A heavy-duty mixer is helpful but not essential for beating cake batter and frosting. An electric hand-held beater is useful for beating small quantities of egg whites, whipping cream, and light batters.

Food Processor: A food processor is useful for chopping and melting chocolate in combination with hot liquids (see page 18). Despite the cleanup, this is the speediest and easiest way to melt and blend chocolate with other ingredients. A processor is the best choice for chopping nuts and dried dates and for grinding cookies finely. A blender may be substituted, but with less satisfactory results. Or, use a chef's knife for chopping and a rolling pin for grinding.

Food Storage Bags: I use 1-gallon size, clear polyethylene non-self-sealing food storage bags for forming chocolate clay flower petals, cutting chocolate with neat rounded edges, and for other specific tasks. Heavy-weight self-sealing plastic bags are ideal for storing leftover chocolate and for keeping chocolate clay malleable.

Measuring Cups and Spoons: Nested measuring cups come in graduated sizes for measuring dry ingredients. Ideally, you should have two sets. To get an accurate measurement, mound the cup slightly above the rim, then level it with a straight blade. Spoon flour into the cup instead of scooping it up with the cup. Measure liquid ingredients in glass or plastic cups that have a handle, a pouring spout, and lines marked on the side indicating various measures. Fill the cup to the desired mark, place it on a counter, and read it at eye level to assure an accurate measure. You should have two 1-cup measuring cups and at least one larger cup. You will also need a set of measuring spoons in graduated sizes.

Metal Spatulas: These practical tools are used for leveling measuring cups and spoons, spreading fillings between cake layers, applying and smoothing frostings, releasing dry piped chocolate designs from waxed paper, and lifting and transferring cakes and chocolate figures from one place to another. They come in two sizes: 8 inches long with a 4-by-¾-inch flat stainless steel blade and a 4-inch-long wooden handle, and 11 inches long with a 6-by-1-inch blade, which is perfect for bigger jobs. All spatula blades should be fairly stiff (test them by bending them), with blunt edges and a rounded end. They are available with straight or angled blades. The bend in the angled blade allows you to grasp the spatula by the handle and spread batter or melted chocolate evenly over a large surface without dragging your knuckles in it. Since spatulas are so important, you should have several small ones and one large one. I prefer an angled spatula for most tasks, but I use a straight blade for frosting cakes. The best spatulas are made by Wilton Enterprises and Ateco.

Microwave-Safe Containers: Using the right kind of container lessens the risk of overheating chocolate in the microwave. Conduct this simple test from Welch and Goodbody's *Unbelievable Microwave Desserts* before using any bowl for the first time: Place the empty bowl in the microwave with 1 cup of water. Microwave on high (100 percent) power for 1 minute; the water should feel hot. If the bowl still feels cool, it is acceptable to use with chocolate. If it feels hot, don't use it. Rubbermaid and Tupperware make excellent microwave-safe, flat-bottomed plastic bowls that I prefer over comparable glass containers.

Mixing Bowls: You can never have too many mixing bowls. Besides using them for mixing batters and tempering chocolate, you should reserve at least one metal or plastic one for molding edible chocolate bowls. The most useful sizes are 4-cup, 6-cup, 8-cup, and 3-quart metal, plastic, or glass bowls. I also recommend using an 8-quart shallow bowl with a 12-inch diameter for folding ingredients into batters. Using a bowl with a large circumference, rather than a deep, narrow bowl, makes it easier to fold delicate mixtures together.

Parchment Paper: Use parchment paper to line baking pans to prevent sticking—thereby eliminating the messy job of greasing the pan. It comes in sheets, rolls, and convenient ready-cut circles that match cake pan sizes. Parchment paper is also sold in pre-cut triangles, specifically made for rolling into cone-shaped decorating bags. I recommend using 15-inch triangles for most chocolate work. These are available in houseware departments and cake decorating supply shops. Rolls of parchment are sold in supermarkets.

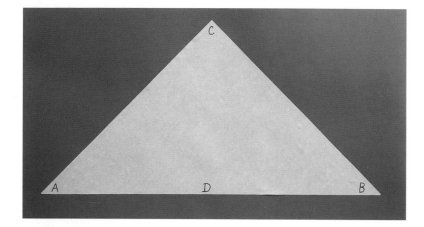

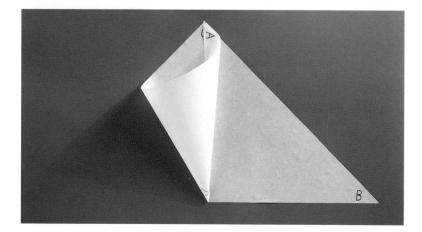

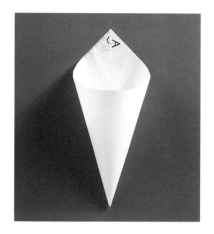

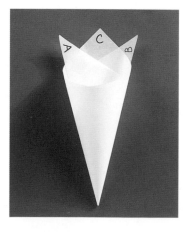

Making a Parchment Bag:

Learning to shape a parchment decorating bag can be frustrating at times, but by the time you have made a dozen bags you should have the technique perfected. To make triangles from a 15-inch sheet of parchment paper, fold the paper diagonally in half, forming a right angle. Using a sharp knife, cut along the fold to form 2 triangles.

1. Label the center of the hypotenuse (the longest side) of a parchment triangle D and the point directly opposite it C. Label the left point of the triangle A and the right point B.

2. Hold the triangle at position D with one hand. Take hold of point A with the other hand and bring it forward, curling the point under itself and placing it directly on top of point C to begin to form the cone.

3. Hold the cone in one hand with the open end up. Bring point B over and around to the back of the cone, aligning it so that all 3 points meet as one.

4. To reinforce the back seam, hold the cone in a horizontal position with the open end facing you. Slide points A and B in opposite directions no further than 1½ inches apart. You should have 3 points visible in the back. If properly made, the opening of the bag should measure approximately 3½ to 4 inches in diameter at the top. Narrower bags have a smaller capacity.

5. Examine the tip of the cone to be sure that it is tightly closed. If it isn't, hold points A and C firmly in place with one hand while pulling point B toward you with the other hand. It also may be necessary to adjust point A; ideally, all 3 points should be even for a tight closure.

continued

6. Secure the seam with a small piece of cellophane tape placed about 2 inches from the tip of the bag. To make a small decorating bag, cut the triangle in half from point D to point C and proceed to roll as directed.

Filling and Closing a Parchment Bag

1. To fill the bag, hold it with one hand, close to the bowl of chocolate, or prop it in a tall, narrow container, taking care not to damage the tip. Using a spoon or small rubber spatula, ladle about ½ cup of chocolate into the bag, filling it only *half full*. Capacities vary according to the size of the bag, so be careful. If you overfill the bag, it will leak and make a mess.

2. To close the bag, press the front and back together, fold the two sides inward, and roll the top portion of the bag down 2 or 3 turns to enclose the chocolate.

3. Grasp the top of the bag firmly with your palm, as if it were a ball, scrunching the rolled top to compress the enclosed chocolate, conforming its shape to your grasp. See page 74 for instructions for using a parchment bag.

Reusable Cleaning Cloths: I find reusable cleaning cloths like Handi Wipes absolutely indispensable for keeping things tidy while I work. They are thin and durable, even when rinsed repeatedly in hot water, and they are disposable, requiring no laundering. Substitute old cleaning cloths, if you must, but I find them cumbersome, less sanitary than Handi Wipes, and more trouble than they are worth.

Rubber Spatulas: The only way to stir a bowl of chocolate properly is with a rubber spatula—not with a stiff (or flimsy) plastic spatula or a wooden spoon. My favorite spatula is 8 inches long with a 6-inch-long handle embedded in a 3½-by-2-inch semiflexible rubber tongue. The curved edge of the tongue allows you to scrape the sides of the bowl cleanly, which is critical when you work with tempered chocolate. You should have three small rubber spatulas and one large one, about 13 by ½ by 2¾ inches, for mixing larger quantities. I recommend Rubbermaid spatulas.

Scale: A scale is an absolute necessity for measuring chocolate, since it is virtually impossible to measure chopped chocolate accurately in a cup. Select one with a large, flat weighing surface that will weigh up to 5 pounds. Terraillon and Krups are popular brands.

Scissors: Scissors are used to cut openings in the tips of parchment decorating bags, to redesign the shapes of fresh leaves, and for many other purposes. I prefer small, sharp-pointed ones.

Sifters, Strainers, and Sieves: Most of the baking recipes in this book call for sifting some of the dry ingredients before you measure them, for which I use a single-mesh strainer. Hold a strainer filled with flour, cocoa, or confectioners' sugar over a sheet of waxed paper and tap it lightly with the heel of your hand to coax the dry ingredients through it.

Strainers or sieves can also be used to strain lumps from chocolate glazes, overheated chocolate, and confectionery coating, and bits of coagulated egg from puddings.

Thermometers: For chocolate work, it is imperative that you have—and use—a thermometer with a range of at least 70° to 130°F. I use a 12-inch-long glass laboratory-type thermometer with easy-to-read 1-degree increments made by Component Design, NW, Inc. An instant-read dial-face thermometer can also be used, but because its sensor is located about 1 ½ inches up from the tip of the stem, it is difficult to accurately measure the temperature of small amounts of chocolate with it.

Candy thermometers are made for cooking sugar syrups (see page 54) to high temperatures. You may already have a mercury thermometer, mounted on stainless steel, that clips to the side of a pan. Test its accuracy by placing it in a saucepan filled with cold water and bringing it to a boil. It should register 212°F if you are at sea level. If slightly inaccurate, factor in the difference. For example, if it registers 214°F at boiling, and the recipe says to cook the syrup to 300°F, cook it to 302°F. If you live at an elevation where water boils at, say, 200°F, you would cook it to 288°F. Thermometers are sold in cookware shops and through mail-order catalogs.

Waxed Paper, Polycoated Freezer Paper, and Acetate Strips:
Waxed paper is good for eliminating cleanup chores, preventing dipped chocolates from adhering to unlined surfaces, lining cake pans and work surfaces, and for many more purposes. Polycoated freezer paper, which is normally used to wrap meat and fish in airtight packages before freezing, can be used to loop, roll, twist, and shape chocolate into bows, tubes, cones, and many other decorative forms, all with a beautiful luster. It is available in the paper-goods section of most supermarkets. Acetate (Mylar) works like freezer paper, except that it gives chocolate an even shinier surface. Strips of acetate are sold in some cake decorating stores and through mail-order catalogs. Sheets of it can be found in most art and office supply stores.

Wire Cake Racks: Baked goods should cool on an elevated wire rack to allow air to circulate under them. You should have at least two racks. Choose one with horizontal wires and another with wires that form a grid. Both types are available in cookware shops and through mail-order catalogs.

SPECIALTY TOOLS

Artists' Brushes: I use a variety of sable hair, acrylic, and watercolor brushes for chocolate work. They include a No. 000 for brush embroidery work (see page 99), and a No. 00, a No. 0, and other assorted watercolor brushes for applying gold luster dust (see page 14) and for other incidental tasks. All are available at art supply stores.

Chocolate Chippers: Chippers were really designed to chop blocks of ice, but today they are more commonly used for chopping chocolate. My favorite is 7 ½ inches long with a 4-inch wooden handle attached to an aluminum bar containing six 1-inch-long sharp prongs. They are available in restaurant supply stores and through specialty mail-order catalogs.

Chocolate Molds: Commercially manufactured chocolate molds are made of metal or transparent plastic materials that are tasteless, odorless, and approved for use with food products. Two types are available: hollow (for making three-dimensional figures) and flat (for making figures with a flat back and a dimensional upper surface). Molds come in many different sizes and designs. They are available in cake and candy supply shops, cookware shops, and through antique dealers.

Every kitchen is filled with other items that are perfect for molding chocolate. Look for metal or food-grade plastic bowls, cookie cutters, cake pans, baking sheets, trays and platters, and disposable cups and plates. All containers for molding should have shiny, scratch-free surfaces with no lips, ridges, or other protrusions inside to inhibit the release of the chocolate.

Cookie Cutters: Cutters can be used to form chocolate and chocolate clay shapes that can be appliquéd on cakes and chocolate boxes and plates. Look for small cutters with simple designs. I also like to use gum paste cutters, which come in beautiful shapes and dainty sizes. Both types are sold in cake decorating shops and through specialty mail-order catalogs.

Corrugated Cake Boards: Corrugated cake boards are placed under cakes to enable you to lift them, coat them with icing, cover the sides with nuts, and then position them on serving plates with very little cleanup. I can't imagine icing or decorating a cake without one! Cake boards placed under chocolate plates and containers enable you to move them without touching the chocolate or soiling the tablecloth. They come in standard square and round cake pan sizes and are available wherever cake decorating equipment is sold.

Decorating Tips and Couplers: Decorating tips are identified by numbers that indicate the size and shape of the opening and/or the size of the tip itself. Generally, the lower the number in each category, the smaller the opening. The round-opening tips used in this book include No. 1, No. 10, No. 12, and a large size No. 1A, which has a ½-inch opening.

A coupler is a threaded nozzle that is inserted into the pastry bag and protrudes through the narrow opening of the bag. A small-size decorating tip is then attached to it from the outside of the bag and held in place with a coupler ring. This allows you to change tips in the middle of a procedure without having to empty the bag. It is practical to have one plastic coupler per pastry bag (see pages 14–15). Large-size tubes like No. 1A are inserted into the bag without a coupler.

Dipping Forks: Dipping forks hold pieces of candy while they are being coated with melted chocolate. Professional ones are about 8 inches long with a 4-inch wooden handle. Attached to each handle is a 4-inch-long stainless steel wire ending in 2, 3, or 4 tines for dipping candies of various shapes and sizes. Others have round, oval, or curled loops instead of tines for dipping truffles and bonbons. They are available through specialty mail-order catalogs. If you can't find them, substitute regular dinner forks with long, narrow tines.

Electric Heating Pad: An electric heating pad, covered with sheets of plastic wrap, can be used to help keep a bowl of tempered chocolate warm while you work. It must be set at its lowest setting and the chocolate monitored carefully, however. If you leave a bowl of chocolate on a heating pad for more than 2 or 3 minutes at a time, it is likely to overheat.

Food Coloring: Chocolate is incompatible with small amounts of water and/or alcohol and will "seize" (tighten into a thick lump) if they are mixed together. That's why you should only use food-safe oil-based candy colors, gels (formerly known as pastes), or powdered food colorings to dye white chocolate or confectionery coating. These are available in cake decorating shops and through specialty mail-order catalogs.

Gloves: My dentist once shared a box of latex medical gloves with me (in exchange for chocolate), and I have been using them ever since to roll and hand dip truffles and other confections in chocolate. These thin, snug-fitting latex gloves are sold in pharmacies and medical supply stores. Cotton "editing" gloves, useful for handling chocolate confections to avoid smudging their shiny surfaces, are sold in photography shops.

Ice Cream Scoops: These scoops are made for portioning out balls of ice cream but they can also be used to form mounds of ganache for truffles. The spring in the handle makes it easy to eject the ganache on a waxed paper–lined baking sheet. These scoops come in several sizes, the number indicating the number of scoops per quart. I recommend No. 100 and No. 200. They are available in cookware shops and through specialty mail-order catalogs.

Luster Dusts: These dusting powders come in a wide range of colors and are applied to chocolate surfaces with a brush to add lustrous accents. The dusts are nontoxic, so they won't hurt you if you ingest them, but their real purpose is decorative, so use them sparingly. Apply the dusts dry with a brush or mixed with alcohol (gin, vodka, or other white spirits) to paint and highlight chocolate designs. Super Gold Luster Dust is one of my favorites.

Marble Slabs: Marble is traditionally used in candy kitchens to cool melted chocolate and hot sugar mixtures for making toffee and other cooked confections. Inexpensive scrap pieces of marble or granite may be purchased at a monument yard (usually located across the street from a cemetery) or from a company that makes custom bathroom vanities. An 18-by-24-inch piece is sufficiently large for most purposes. If you don't have a piece of marble, substitute a laminated Corian or Formica countertop for chocolate and confectionery coating work, but use a heavy metal baking sheet to cool hot sugar mixtures.

Melon-Ball Cutters: These cutters, which are normally used to form melon balls, can also be used to shape mounds of ganache to form truffles. A handle in the center of the cutter is attached to 1-inch and ¾-inch cups at each end. To use the cutter, scrape the cup against the surface of firm ganache and drop the mound on a waxed paper–lined baking sheet. Melon-ball cutters are available in houseware departments and cookware shops.

Pasta Machine: A pasta machine does a fine job of flattening and cutting thin sheets of chocolate clay for making ribbons, bows, nests, bands, ruffles, and many other decorative items. Standard manual machines are available in cookware shops and through most specialty mail-order catalogs.

Pastry Bags: Pastry bags can be used to pipe frosting and whipped cream decorations onto fancy cakes and desserts or to perform utilitarian tasks like piping out mounds of truffle mixture on a baking sheet. Lightweight, flexible polyester pastry bags come in sizes from 8 to 18 inches. Until you are more experienced, I recommend buying a 10- and 12-inch bag. My favorite bags, made by Wilton Enterprises, are soft, malleable, and form to the shape of your hand easily. They are often used in combination with a plastic coupler, which allows you to attach and detach the decorating tip from the outside of the bag, even when the inside is full of icing. Large decorating tips are placed directly into the bag without a coupler.

The narrow opening of a new bag must be cut to fit the coupler before you can use it. Measure and cut off a ¾-inch piece and insert the nozzle end of the coupler, pushing it down as far as it will go with your thumb to see how much more needs to be cut. Remove the nozzle and keep cutting until just one or two threads of the coupler show on the outside of the bag.

Preparing and Filling a Pastry Bag

To prepare the bag for use, insert the nozzle part of the coupler into the narrow end of the bag. Attach the decorating tip to the end of the coupler and secure it with the coupler ring.

To fill the bag, cuff the top of the bag over the rim of a tall, narrow container to make it easier to handle, or hold the cuffed bag in your hand. Using a spoon or a spatula, fill the bag half full of frosting or whipped cream. Press the spatula against the side of the bag as you pull it out, keeping the frosting deep in the bag. Uncuff the top and, using your thumb and index finger, push down on the outside to compress the frosting. Twist the bag tightly closed above the filled portion. Cradle it in the palm of your hand with your thumb and forefinger securing the twisted part in a locked position, leaving the rest of your fingers free to press on the bag. Steady your working hand by placing the index finger of your free hand near the coupler end of the bag, with your elbows close to the body or braced against the work surface.

Pattern Boards: I use pattern boards constantly throughout this book for piping chocolate designs over predrawn patterns, for practicing new piping skills, and for transferring dipped confections from one place to another. To make them, cut a 13-by-19-inch corrugated cake rectangle in half to form two 13-by-9 ½-inch pieces. Cover each board with a sheet of waxed paper cut an inch or so wider than the board. Fold the sides over and tape them on the back. Leave the short ends of the board open so that you can slide a pattern sheet under the paper. You can substitute rimless or inverted sided baking sheets lined with waxed paper, if necessary. Rimless baking sheets do not need to be inverted.

Polishing Brush: Confectioners use soft brushes to buff imperfections off chocolate surfaces. Professional ones are made of soft badger, camel, or squirrel hair, the wider the better. Comparable brushes are sometimes available in art supply stores. For best results, let chocolate return to room temperature before stroking it briskly with a brush in one direction only.

Scriber Tool: This sharp-pointed tool is used to mark designs on royal icing and to etch patterns on chocolate. It is available in cake decorating stores and through specialty mail-order catalogs. Substitute a long nail or a darning needle.

Square-Notched Adhesive Spreader: Inexpensive plastic adhesive spreaders made for installing floor and wall tiles can be used to create a two-tone striped design on bands of chocolate and other chocolate pieces. They are available in the home-improvement section of most hardware stores.

Wall Scrapers: Wall scrapers made for scraping wallpaper off walls and applying wall putty can also be used to spread thin layers of chocolate onto a marble surface and to make curls, bands, and ruffles. I recommend Warner or Ace Hardware brand scrapers with a black 4 ¾-inch plastic handle and a *flexible* stainless steel blade with a blunt edge. You will need 3- and 6-inch-wide scrapers. They are available in the home-improvement section of most hardware stores.

2

melting and tempering chocolate

Working with chocolate is fun—provided you handle it properly. Unfortunately, not everybody does, which is why chocolate has developed a reputation for being temperamental and too technically demanding for the average home cook. I hope to dispel misconceptions like this by providing you with accurate information and easy-to-follow, technically sound techniques for melting and tempering chocolate, the two most misunderstood skills related to chocolate work.

melting chocolate

There is more than one way to melt a bar of chocolate. As a traveling cooking teacher, I've been caught without a stove or a microwave and have had to resort to some unusual heat sources. I've used a heating pad, an electric hot tray, an infrared heat lamp, a gooseneck lamp with a 100-watt bulb, and a hair dryer, but the most unusual method I ever used was solar energy. When the power went out during one of my classes in Chihuahua, Mexico, we put our bowls of chocolate in a sunny window and, voilà: The chocolate was melted in record time.

Many of the problems attributed to chocolate's "cranky disposition" are really the result of improper melting procedures. If you follow these simple guidelines, your chocolate will melt smoothly every time:

Chop the chocolate into almond-sized pieces. It will melt faster and more evenly. Thin bars are easy to break up by hand. Use a chipper (see page 12) or a heavy French chef's knife to chop thicker bars. Confectionery coating and some brands of chocolate are sold in wafer, chip, and bite-sized rectangular shapes that don't require chopping.

Always melt chocolate slowly, at a low temperature. The melting point of chocolate (between 86° and 96° F) is lower than body temperature (98.6° F), which is why a small piece of chocolate melts in your mouth or in your hand so quickly. The melting point of confectionery coating is slightly higher. Using high heat is risky and the most common cause of grainy and/or lumpy chocolate or confectionery coating.

Never heat dark chocolate or confectionery coating above 120° F. Milk and white chocolates, which are more heat sensitive, should not be heated above 110° F. (If overheated, the milk proteins they contain cook and form clumps, causing lumpy chocolate.) A good test is to hold the bowl with the chocolate in the palm of your hand; it should never feel too hot to touch. If it's too hot for your hand, it's too hot for the chocolate.

Begin stirring the chocolate with a rubber spatula when the outside edges of the chocolate start to liquefy. Stirring prematurely actually slows down the melt.

Chocolate retains its shape in the microwave as it melts, so don't rely on appearance alone. The only way to know if it's fully melted is to stir it.

MELTING CHOCOLATE IN A HOT-WATER BATH

This popular method utilizes hot—not steaming, simmering, or boiling—water to melt chopped chocolate. Steam escaping from the sides of the pan or condensation of any kind can cause the chocolate to *seize*, or *tighten*, two words that perfectly describe what happens when melted chocolate suddenly turns into a hard lump. The same thing will happen if you accidentally splash a little water into the chocolate.

To melt 1 pound or more of chocolate, you'll need a conventional double boiler or a stainless steel bowl that fits snugly over the top of a saucepan (my preference). To melt smaller amounts, use a glass measuring cup placed in a shallow pan half-filled with hot water.

1. Using a chocolate chipper or a heavy French chef's knife, chop the chocolate into almond-sized pieces.

2. Fill the bottom pan with enough hot water (130° to 140°F), drawn from the tap or heated briefly, to touch the bottom of the top bowl when it is in place, but not so much as to allow it to float. If you heat the water on the stove, be sure to do so *before* the top bowl is in place, *never* while it is over the water.

3. Place ⅓ of the chocolate in a bowl (or the top of the double boiler) and position it over the hot-water bath. Let the chocolate begin to melt before stirring it with a rubber spatula. Add the rest of the chocolate gradually, allowing each addition to melt before adding the next. Stir frequently to distribute the heat evenly. If the water cools before the chocolate is completely melted, set the bowl or top of the double boiler aside while you replace or reheat the water and continue the melting process.

4. Carefully lift the bowl from the water bath as soon as the chocolate is nearly melted (especially if it's milk or white chocolate). Dry the bottom and place it on the work surface. Continue stirring until it is smooth and shiny.

MICROWAVE TIMETABLE FOR MELTING CHOCOLATE

(Medium or 50 percent power)

Amount of Chocolate	Time
1 ounce	1 minute
2 ounces	1 minute and 30 seconds
4 ounces	2 minutes and 15 seconds
6 ounces	2 minutes and 30 seconds
8 ounces	3 minutes
1 pound	3 minutes and 15 seconds
1 ½ pounds	3 minutes and 30 seconds
2 pounds	4 minutes and 15 seconds
2 ½ pounds	4 minutes and 30 seconds
3 pounds	4 minutes and 45 seconds

MELTING CHOCOLATE IN A MICROWAVE OVEN

The microwave does a quick and efficient job of melting chocolate and has become one of my favorite methods. Choosing the right container, however, is critical to success. Be sure to conduct the test on page 9 to determine whether your bowl is safe to use. Bowls that remain cool or slightly warm after microwaving are the most desirable. Those that retain heat can scorch the chocolate in a matter of moments. If you *do* overheat the chocolate, immediately transfer it to another bowl, deposit some chunks of solid chocolate into it, and stir, stir, stir.

Many microwave ovens are equipped with a turntable that rotates when the oven is on. If yours doesn't have one, stir the chocolate and rotate the bowl manually one-quarter turn every 60 seconds after the first minute of microwaving and even more frequently toward the end.

It is next to impossible to provide a definitive time chart for melting chocolate in a microwave, but the range of times on the preceding page, tested in a 900-watt microwave oven using medium (50 percent) power, will serve as a guide. Don't take the chart for gospel, however; first test the suggested times for yourself using *your* microwave, *your* chocolate, and *your* containers. Be sure to record your findings for future reference.

1. Using a chocolate chipper or a heavy French chef's knife, chop 1 to 8 ounces of chocolate into almond-sized pieces.

2. Place the chocolate in a microwave-safe bowl that is large enough to accommodate the quantity of chocolate to be melted. Microwave uncovered on medium (50 percent) power for 1 to 3 minutes, depending on the amount. Using a rubber spatula, stir the chocolate gently at the halfway mark.

3. Continue microwaving in increasingly shorter time increments until most, but not all, of the chocolate is melted. Put the bowl on the work surface and continue stirring until the chocolate is smooth and shiny and all the pieces are melted.

MELTING CHOCOLATE WITH LIQUID INGREDIENTS

Recipes often call for melting chocolate with milk, cream, water, butter, or a combination of liquids. Doing so often saves steps, reduces the chances of overheating the chocolate, and even speeds the actual melting time.

Chocolate has a love/hate relationship with liquid, however: It loves a lot and hates a little. Recipes that call for melting chocolate with liquid should always allow at least 1 tablespoon of liquid for every 2 ounces of chocolate to prevent the dry particles of cocoa and sugar in the chocolate from clumping together, forming a thick lump. Dark couverture chocolates (see page 3), which contain the most cocoa solids, may require a little more liquid, so be ready to add 1 extra tablespoon of liquid or more if the chocolate shows signs of thickening.

COMBINING CHOPPED CHOCOLATE WITH HOT LIQUID

Recipes for truffles and glazes often suggest adding chopped chocolate to a pan of hot (scalded) cream or pouring hot cream over chopped chocolate to melt it. The cool pieces of chocolate lower the temperature of the hot liquid instantly, before it can overheat the chocolate, and the hot cream melts the chocolate.

When adding hot liquid to chopped chocolate, be sure to add it all at once. Adding small amounts of liquid at a time may cause the chocolate to thicken, rather than liquefy. Stirring or whisking the chocolate will speed the melt by dispersing the heat evenly. One popular method suggests combining chopped chocolate with hot liquid in the food processor. To do so, place the chocolate in the bowl of the processor and secure the top. With the machine running, pour a steady stream of hot liquid down the feed tube in the lid. The whirling action will mix the ingredients, disperse the heat, and melt the chocolate in a matter of seconds. The same thing can be done in an electric mixer set at a low speed to prevent splashing.

MELTING CONFECTIONERY COATING

Confectionery coating may be melted in a hot-water bath, just as chocolate is. You will need to take extra care if you melt it in the microwave, however. Confectionery coating contains more sugar than chocolate, so it scorches more easily. When microwaving confectionery coating, stir it frequently, using shorter time increments than those given for chocolate (see previous page).

COMBINING MELTED CHOCOLATE WITH COLD INGREDIENTS

Combining melted chocolate with cold ingredients like whipped cream can be tricky. Cocoa butter begins to solidify at 75° F, so if you combine cool chocolate with cold cream, portions of the cocoa butter will solidify on contact, causing the chocolate to turn chunky. To help prevent that, add at least 1 tablespoon of tepid water or cream to every 2 ounces of melted chocolate. Doing so will "loosen" the chocolate, making it more fluid and easier to fold into the cream (see page 138).

SALVAGING CHOCOLATE MISTAKES

Like bad-hair days, sooner or later everyone who works with chocolate has a bad-chocolate day. To rescue overheated chocolate that has thickened and/or become lumpy, add some smooth, freshly melted chocolate combined with a few drops of soya liquid lecithin (available in natural foods stores). Adding 1 teaspoon flavorless vegetable oil or melted homogenized vegetable shortening (Crisco) per pound of overheated chocolate also may help. Sometimes it's simpler just to strain the chocolate or whirl it in the food processor until smooth. Lumpy white chocolate may be caused by moisture acquired during storage. To salvage it, proceed with the same directions.

To cool chocolate that has been overheated, immediately remove the bowl from the heat source, transfer the chocolate to a cool bowl, deposit some chunks of solid chocolate into it, and stir constantly. The longer the chocolate remains overheated, the less chance there is to salvage it. It is a lost cause once the chocolate hardens.

If you overheat confectionery coating, immediately transfer it to another bowl, deposit a handful of confectionery coating pieces into it, and stir, stir, stir. Or, add a few drops of soya liquid lecithin or 1 teaspoon melted homogenized vegetable shortening per pound.

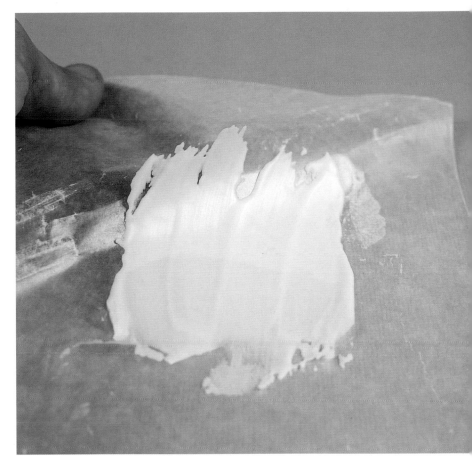

❧ Smearing the chocolate to test the temper, page 24.

tempering chocolate

If you want to make professional-quality truffles, mold fancy shapes, or pipe decorative designs, then you must first learn to *temper* melted chocolate. Tempering is a heating, cooling, and stirring process that induces melted chocolate to set with a glossy surface and smooth texture. Tempering is *not* required when you're going to use chocolate as an ingredient in cake batters, cookie doughs, mousses, truffle centers, chocolate clay, and other recipes.

ABOUT TEMPERING

When chocolate is heated, all of the cocoa butter melts and no cocoa butter crystals remain. As the cocoa butter cools, if stirred, it begins to form cocoa butter crystals. One form is stable, while others are not. Tempering creates the conditions needed to maintain the stable (good) cocoa butter crystals and eliminate the unstable (bad) ones.

Melted chocolate that has been tempered sets quickly, releases from molds easily, and holds its shape when you pipe designs with it. When it solidifies, its surface is glossy and unblemished—even at room temperature—enabling you to make decorations and confections in advance without having to keep them refrigerated until shortly before serving. Tempered chocolate snaps when you break it and resists softening when you touch it. Its interior is equally firm, smooth, and uniform in color.

Untempered melted chocolate sets slowly, sticks to molds, and does not hold its shape well when you pipe with it. When it solidifies, untempered chocolate has a dull surface, usually blemished with gray streaks and blotches (bloom). It is soft and crumbly when you break it, sometimes revealing gray layers on the inside.

Manufacturers always temper their chocolate before it leaves the factory, and, with proper handling and storage, it is still in temper when you buy it. Once you melt it, however, the tempering process must usually be repeated to assure that the melted cocoa butter crystals will recrystallize in stable form again so that you can use the chocolate for molding, coating, and piping.

I am always disappointed when I read instructions that suggest doing all kinds of fancy things with melted chocolate but fail to mention anything about tempering. Such instructions are misleading and almost always result in disappointment. It is equally disheartening to see the tempering process described in very technical terms, as if being a rocket scientist were a prerequisite for working with chocolate.

The following points will help to clarify the tempering process:

The tempering process always begins by melting the chocolate. If the chocolate is *in temper* (glossy and smooth textured) before you melt it, you do not have to heat it to any precise temperature (so long as you don't exceed the maximum 120°F). If it is *out of temper* (dull, blemished, or grainy), you must heat it to 110° (milk or white chocolate) or 115°F (dark chocolate). Untempered chocolate contains unstable cocoa butter crystals that will not melt until they reach those temperatures. If you do not eliminate the unstable crystals during the melting step, they will sabotage your tempering efforts.

A thermometer is essential when working with chocolate (see page 12). Tempering requires precise temperature control. While it is true that many experienced people can temper chocolate by "feel," using a thermometer is a much more reliable method. Position the thermometer in the center of the bowl of melted chocolate without touching the bottom or sides, or any chunks of chocolate. Wait at least 1 minute before reading its temperature to give it time to register properly.

Dark chocolate is easier to temper than milk and white chocolates because of the milk solids the latter contain. I suggest you start with dark chocolate and then move on to the others.

Melt and temper more chocolate than you think you'll need, unless you plan to use it all at one time. The more chocolate in the bowl, the slower it cools, and the longer you'll be able to work with it before it needs rewarming. Having extra chocolate also lessens the risk of running short in the middle of a project. Leftover chocolate is reusable.

Use a rubber spatula, not a metal or wooden spoon, to stir the chocolate during the tempering process and to scrape the sides of the bowl to keep the cooler chocolate from solidifying there once the chocolate is in temper.

Learn to recognize the physical changes that occur during the tempering process so that, with experience, you will be able to *see* when the chocolate is ready to be used. Untempered melted chocolate is fluid and shiny, like patent leather. As it nears the tempered state, it becomes noticeably thicker and somewhat lighter in color, with a lustrous, satiny sheen, signs that the cocoa butter is cooling and forming stable crystals.

The best range for working with tempered dark chocolate is 86° to 90° F. The best range for working with milk or white chocolate is 84° to 88° F. The chocolate is still in temper below those ranges, but it may require warming.

Chocolate is forgiving. If at first you don't succeed, remelt your mistakes and try again.

TEMPERING METHODS

There are three common methods for tempering chocolate: the chunk method, the controlled method, and the classic method. Here is a summary of each, and full instructions follow.

Chunk Method: Melt the chocolate; if it is not in temper, melt milk and white chocolates to 110° F and dark chocolate to 115° F. Add chunks of solid tempered chocolate. Stir to lower the temperature to less than 90° F for dark chocolate (88° F for milk and white chocolates). Remove the chunks. The chocolate is now in temper and ready to be tested and used.

Controlled Method: (To be used only with tempered chocolate.) *Partially* melt the chocolate, removing it from the heat source before the temperature exceeds 90° F for dark chocolate (88° F for milk and white chocolates). Stir to complete the melt. The chocolate is *still* in temper and ready to be tested and used.

If you exceed the specified temperatures, add chunks of solid tempered chocolate and stir to lower the temperature to less than 90° F for dark chocolate (88° F for milk and white chocolates). Remove the chunks. The chocolate is now in temper and ready to be tested and used.

Classic Method: Melt the chocolate; if it is not in temper, melt milk and white chocolates to 110° F and dark chocolate to 115° F. Remove from the heat source and, stirring frequently, let cool to 84° F for dark chocolate and 82° F for milk and white chocolates. Rewarm the chocolate to less than 90° F for dark chocolate (88° F for milk and white chocolates). The chocolate is now in temper and ready to be tested and used.

Chunk Tempering Method

One of the simplest ways to temper chocolate is to drop a few chunks of tempered chocolate into a bowl of melted chocolate, stir them, and watch what happens. It doesn't take long for the chunks, which are full of stable cocoa butter crystals, to begin to melt, flooding the bowl with the same kind of crystals that the chocolate needs to regain its temper. Those "seed" crystals work fast, and before long, the whole bowl is full of stable cocoa butter crystals and the chocolate is ready to use.

1 pound semisweet chocolate coarsely chopped, plus 4 ounces semisweet chocolate, in chunks (see Notes)

1. Clear a 2-foot-wide area of work surface. Have at hand a rubber spatula, a thermometer, a dampened reusable cloth to wipe it clean, and a sheet of waxed paper.

2. Melt the chopped chocolate (see page 16). If the chocolate is not in temper before you melt it, melt milk and white chocolates to 110° F and dark chocolate to 115° F. Remove it from the heat source. If necessary, let cool to 100° F.

3. Add the chocolate chunks. Submerge them in the chocolate with a rubber spatula. Turn them over frequently, stirring gently and moving them all around the bowl, making contact with the entire melted mass. When the bottom of the bowl feels cool and the chocolate appears to be thickening, insert the thermometer into the center of the bowl. If the chocolate is less than 90° F (88° F for milk and white chocolates), the chocolate is ready to be tested and used (see page 24). If it's still too warm, stir and cool it longer. Remove the thermometer, wipe it clean, and set it aside.

4. Using the rubber spatula, scoop out whatever is left of the partially melted chunks and place them on a sheet of waxed paper. Don't overlook any pieces, or they will continue to cool the chocolate and cause it to become lumpy. Refrigerate the chunks for 10 minutes and store them in an airtight container at room temperature for future use. The chocolate is now ready to be tested and used (see page 24).

Chocolate Notes

Never "seed" a bowl of chocolate with *untempered* chunks of chocolate, because they contain *unstable* cocoa butter crystals. Adding them to the chocolate would do the opposite of what is desired.

It doesn't matter what size chunks of chocolate you use to temper a bowl of chocolate so long as they are large enough to retrieve easily from the melted chocolate at the end of the tempering process. I often use 2-inch chunks.

The total weight of the chunks should be about one-fourth the weight of the melted chocolate. For example, use 4 ounces of chocolate chunks to "seed" 1 pound of melted chocolate, 8 ounces to "seed" 2 pounds of melted chocolate, and 12 ounces to "seed" 3 pounds of melted chocolate (see page 157). The chunks are reusable for the same purpose, or you can melt them down (or eat them).

To achieve the proper tempering results, chunks of chocolate must be present in the bowl when the temperature reaches 90° F (88° F for milk and white chocolates). If you see that you're running out of chunks, add more.

Controlled Tempering Method

This method can only be used with solid chocolate that is in temper before you melt it. It is quick, easy, and almost foolproof, since there is an equally simple and fast solution if something goes wrong.

Glossy, unblemished dark chocolate will begin to lose it temper when it is heated to temperatures over 90°F (88°F for milk and white chocolates). But, if you monitor it carefully as it melts and remove it from the heat source before it reaches that temperature, you can maintain its temper, thereby eliminating the need for further steps (see Note). If you exceed 90°F, simply add a few chunks of tempered chocolate to the bowl and proceed as directed.

Naturally, this method, which relies on maintaining the temper in chocolate through temperature control, will only work if the chocolate is in temper (i.e., glossy and unblemished) before you melt it. It would be unproductive to use this method if the chocolate to be melted is dull and blemished, because you can't maintain the temper in chocolate that has already lost it.

> 1 pound semisweet chocolate, coarsely chopped, plus 4 ounces semisweet chocolate, in chunks, if needed

1. Clear a 2-foot-wide area of work space. Have at hand a rubber spatula, a thermometer, a dampened reusable cloth to wipe it clean, and a sheet of waxed paper.

2. Melt the chopped chocolate (see page 16). If you use the microwave method, use medium (50 percent) power for 3 minutes. Continue melting or microwaving in increasingly shorter time increments, until ⅔ of the chocolate is melted. Remove the bowl from the heat source and put it on the work surface. Using a rubber spatula, stir it gently, coaxing the remaining pieces to melt. If they do not melt, warm the chocolate again very briefly.

3. Check the temperature with a thermometer. If it is less than 90°F (88°F for milk and white chocolates), the chocolate is still in temper and ready to be used. If the temperature is higher, add the chunks of chocolate and stir until the melted chocolate reaches the proper temperature. Remove the thermometer, wipe it clean, and set it aside.

4. Using a rubber spatula, scoop out whatever is left of the chunks and place them on the waxed paper. Refrigerate the chunks for 10 minutes and store in an airtight container at room temperature for future use. The bowl of tempered chocolate is now ready to be tested and used (see page 24).

Chocolate Notes

This controlled method of tempering chocolate stops the melting process *before* all the cocoa butter crystals melt, leaving enough stable cocoa butter crystals in the bowl of melted chocolate to maintain the chocolate's temper. No further steps are necessary.

If you use the microwave chart (see page 17) to melt the chocolate for this tempering method, use slightly less time than what is suggested, followed by shorter time increments, so that you can monitor the chocolate's melting progress more closely as it nears the proper temperature.

Classic Tempering Method

This method produces an exceptional temper in chocolate, but it is more complicated and time-consuming than the previous ones. If you've never tempered chocolate, use an alternative method until you become comfortable with the process. However, if you are caught without chunks of chocolate for "seeding" purposes, this is the method you will have to use.

1 pound semisweet chocolate, coarsely chopped

1. Clear a 2-foot-wide area of work surface. Have at hand a rubber spatula, a thermometer, and a dampened reusable cloth to wipe it clean.

2. Melt the chocolate to 115°F (melt milk and white chocolates to 110°F). Remove the chocolate from the heat source and place it on the work surface. Let cool, stirring occasionally with a rubber spatula, until it reaches 84°F (82°F for milk and white chocolates). To speed the process, place the bowl over a pan or slightly larger bowl of cool water, stirring the chocolate frequently to maintain an even temperature.

3. Now the chocolate must be warmed—carefully. Place the bowl of cool chocolate over a pan or slightly larger bowl filled with 100°F water, or microwave on low (30 percent) power for up to 10 seconds. Stir gently. Continue warming or microwaving (using increasingly shorter time increments for the microwave) and checking the temperature of the chocolate with a thermometer, until it reaches no higher than 90°F (88°F for milk and white chocolates). If you exceed that temperature, you must reheat the chocolate and start all over again. The temperature may be 2° or 3° lower but not higher than that temperature. Set the bowl of chocolate on the counter, remove the thermometer, wipe it clean, and set it aside. The chocolate is now ready to be tested and used (see below).

Chocolate Note
When you only need a small amount of tempered chocolate, pour 1 or 2 ounces of melted chocolate directly onto the work surface and turn it with a 3-inch wall scraper or an angled metal spatula until it feels cool. Use at once.

TESTING THE TEMPER IN CHOCOLATE

To test your tempering prowess before proceeding with any chocolate project, smear a thin sample of the tempered chocolate on a small piece of waxed paper and refrigerate it for 3 to 5 minutes. If, after that amount of time, the sample is dry to the touch and evenly glossy, the chocolate is ready to use. If it isn't, the bowl of chocolate may require further cooling. Stir the chocolate gently, adding another chunk if necessary, and check the temperature again. If the chocolate continues to fail the test, reheat it to 110° to 115°F and start the cooling process all over again.

KEEPING THE TEMPER: YOURS AND CHOCOLATE'S

Tempering a bowl of chocolate is easy, but keeping it warm and fluid while you work with it may require a little extra effort. The first place that the chocolate will begin to cool is along the sides of the bowl, so it is imperative that you periodically scrape the liquid chocolate off the sides with a rubber spatula before it begins to solidify there. If you forget to do that, the adhering chocolate will act as "seed," cooling and thickening the melted chocolate quickly and causing it to become unmanageable. Once that happens, you will have to remelt the chocolate and begin again.

Here are some other preventative measures:

Place a folded towel under the bowl or nest it inside a similar-sized bowl to buffer it from the coolness of the work surface.

Sit the bowl of chocolate in a pan or slightly larger bowl of 90° F water, replenishing the warm water as necessary. Stir the chocolate occasionally, scraping the sides of the bowl.

Sit the bowl of chocolate in a pan or slightly larger bowl of hot (130° to 140° F) water just for *a few seconds*, stirring it to maintain an even temperature.

Periodically warm the bowl of chocolate in the microwave oven on low (30 percent) power, using 10- to 15-second increments. Be careful, for if you exceed the maximum temperature allowed for tempered chocolate (see page 21), you will have to cool it down with a few chunks of chocolate again.

Occasionally place the bowl under a gooseneck lamp fitted with a 100-watt light bulb, stirring occasionally to maintain an even temperature.

Place the bowl on a heating pad protected with several sheets of plastic wrap and set on its lowest setting—just for brief periods. If you leave it there unattended for more than 2 or 3 minutes at a time, it can overheat the chocolate, thereby breaking the temper. Stir the bowl frequently to maintain an even temperature.

The cooler the melted chocolate, the less perfect its temper, and the more difficult it is to use. That's why it's important to try to keep the chocolate warm and fluid while you work with it. Unless you are a purist, however, you can continue to use cool tempered chocolate with good results until it becomes too thick to handle. Tempered chocolate will not lose its temper unless you heat it above the specified temperatures.

AUTOMATIC TEMPERING MACHINES

Until recently, home cooks could only dream about owning a machine, like those used by professional confectioners, that automatically melts and tempers chocolate. Though some people still consider them a luxury, small automatic tempering machines are now becoming quite popular with serious home cooks who want the convenience of having their own little "master confectioner" in the kitchen keeping a bowl of chocolate in temper all day.

There are currently three small machines suitable for home use: the Little Dipper (Hilliard's Chocolate System); the Table Top Temperer (American Chocolate Mould Co., Inc.); and the Sinsation Chocolate Maker (Chandré Corporation). The Little Dipper and the Table Top Temperer are controlled by a thermostat and use two 100-watt light bulbs and a small fan to melt, temper, and keep up to 4 pounds of chocolate at a time at just the right temperature all day, which is a convenience that makes them well worth the money. The Sinsation Chocolate Maker is a state-of-the-art, computer chip–controlled machine that ensures perfect melting and tempering results every time. It is a convenient 12 by 10½ by 5 inches and weighs only 6½ pounds. The removable bowl holds about 1½ pounds of chocolate.

3

spectacular chocolate confections

Eating a chocolate confection is the ultimate form of gratification, an indulgence that you can sink your teeth into and still savor in your memory long after the last of it has melted away.

This chapter contains everything you need to know to create some of the best chocolate confections you've ever eaten. If you follow the step-by-step instructions, use quality ingredients, and select the proper tools, you should have great results, even the first time. Learning to work with chocolate is a cumulative process. What you learn in this chapter will serve as a stepping stone to the next level and to the fancier chocolate creations that lie ahead.

Here are some general tips:

Develop orderly work habits. Read the recipe introduction, the recipe, and the Chocolate Notes that follow it before you start. Review the melting and tempering instructions. Clear a 3-foot-wide area of work surface. Assemble the right equipment. Weigh, measure, chop, and melt everything you're going to need ahead of time.

Bite off only as much as you can chew (so to speak). Select an appropriate recipe for your level of expertise. Start with the easy recipes at the beginning of this chapter, and as you gain experience, gradually work your way through to the end.

Use the best ingredients. It takes just as much time to make a quality product as it does an inferior one, but the results are never equal.

Set aside at least 1 hour of undisturbed attention for the simple recipes and 2 hours for the more complicated ones.

Don't rush things. If the instructions say to cool the chocolate to 90°F, do it. Chocolate is forgiving, but only up to a point.

Practice, practice, practice. The more often you make candy, the better at it you will become, so look for opportunities to make some for friends and family throughout the year. Your skills will improve and so will your stature in the community.

Since chocolate is the primary ingredient and major flavoring agent in many candy recipes, it's important to experiment with different brands to find the one you like best. Don't be misled by hearsay. The only way to judge a chocolate is to put it in your mouth and experience it (see page 5).

The most frequently used chocolates for candy making are bittersweet, semisweet, milk, and white chocolates. In some cases, you can use them interchangeably, but not always. In truffle recipes, for example, you cannot substitute dark chocolate for milk or white chocolate without adjusting the rest of the recipe. When a candy recipe calls for unsweetened cocoa powder, you can use either natural (nonalkalized) or Dutched (alkalized). Natural cocoa will impart the strongest chocolate flavor, while Dutched will supply the darkest color.

Whenever a candy recipe calls for *chocolate*, use real chocolate, not confectionery coating. Chocolate imparts a much stronger flavor in candy centers than coating, for the same amount of effort. Use confectionery coating only in recipes that have been developed specifically for that product, such as Peanut Butter Meltaways (page 52).

❧ Chocolate Caramel Pecan Patties, page 30.

using leftover tempered chocolate

Many of the recipes in this chapter intentionally call for more chocolate than you will actually use. This is not a wasteful suggestion. Experience has taught me that it is more practical—and a lot easier—to work with larger rather than smaller amounts of chocolate. The extra supply of chocolate will extend the time you'll be able to work with it, lessen the risk of running short, and provide the necessary volume required for certain procedures like dipping. Whatever remains is reusable unless you have overheated the chocolate or splashed liquid into it, so why penalize yourself when you can have your chocolate and eat it, too? The simplest way to handle leftover tempered chocolate is to spread it on a sheet of waxed paper, refrigerate it until set, and then store it in an airtight container at a moderate (72°F) room temperature for future use.

MAKING CHOCOLATE BARK

You can use leftover tempered chocolate to make chocolate bark. Simply combine any amount of leftover chocolate with chopped or whole toasted nuts; cut-up dried apricots, cherries, cranberries, raisins, or coconut; dry cereal; or anything else that is crispy or chewy. Using an angled spatula, spread the mixture about ¼ inch thick on a rimless waxed paper–lined baking sheet, using the tines of a fork to rearrange and distribute the chunky pieces. Refrigerate until the bark sets, about 15 minutes. Let sit at room temperature for about 1 hour before cutting it into squares with a large, sharp knife.

When making bark, the proportions you use will determine how chunky the mixture will be. As a rule of thumb, use 1 pound chocolate to 4 ounces (about 1 cup) whole toasted almonds or other additions. These additions will cause the chocolate to cool down fast, so once you've combined everything, you must work quickly, or the chocolate will set before you have time to spread it. Once you gain experience, you will enjoy mixing, matching, and experimenting with different combinations.

MAKING NUT CLUSTERS

Like bark, nut clusters do not require a written recipe. Simply combine any amount of leftover melted and tempered chocolate with nuts, dried fruit, coconut, or other crispy additions. If the texture of the mixture is not chunky enough, add more crunchy stuff. Then, working quickly with 2 teaspoons, place the mixture in fluted paper candy cups or deposit it in small clusters on a rimless waxed paper–lined baking sheet. Refrigerate until set, about 5 minutes.

storing leftover untempered chocolate

It is always better to store leftover chocolate in a tempered state; otherwise, it will set up with a blemished surface and a crumbly texture, and it will have a shorter shelf life. The discoloration will disappear when the chocolate is melted; it can now be used for baking. If the untempered chocolate is to be used for molding or decorative work, however, you must heat it to 110° (milk or white chocolate) or 115°F (dark chocolate) first (to eliminate the unstable cocoa butter crystals that it contains), then retemper it.

Chocolate Medallions

These little confectionery gems were inspired by a gold medallion in my jewelry box. I've substituted an assortment of nuts embedded in chocolate for the precious stones in gold, but unlimited variations are possible just by choosing other nuts, dried fruit, or bits of colorful candy. If you've never worked with tempered chocolate, this recipe is a good introduction. To make a smaller batch, cut the ingredients in half.

¼ cup hazelnuts, toasted and skinned
(see page 7)

⅓ cup pecan halves

½ cup lightly salted cashews

1 pound semisweet chocolate,
coarsely chopped, plus
4 ounces semisweet chocolate,
in chunks (for tempering)

1. Clear a 3-foot-wide area of work surface. Arrange the nuts in separate piles on a small baking sheet. Line a large rimless baking sheet with waxed paper, securing it with tape. Have at hand a regular teaspoon or an iced-tea spoon and an angled metal spatula.

2. Melt and temper the chopped chocolate (see page 16). Holding the bowl close to the baking sheet, scoop out 1 rounded teaspoonful of chocolate, scraping the bottom of the spoon on the edge of the bowl. Let the chocolate roll off the tip of the spoon into a mound in the upper left-hand corner of the baking sheet. Using the tip of the spoon, coax the mound into a 2-inch-round puddle about ⅛ inch thick. To smooth the surface, jiggle it lightly with the tip of the spoon while it's still fluid. Repeat to make 2 or 3 more puddles, spaced 1 inch apart.

3. Embed each puddle with a pecan, a cashew, and a hazelnut before the chocolate sets. Repeat, making 3 or 4 puddles at a time, until all the chocolate and/or nuts are used.

4. Stir the bowl of chocolate occasionally as you work, scraping the sides to keep the cooler chocolate from solidifying on the walls. If the chocolate starts to thicken before you're finished, carefully place it over a bowl of hot water (130° to 140°) for a few seconds or microwave it on low (30 percent) power in 10- to 15-second increments, never letting the temperature exceed 90°F.

5. Refrigerate the medallions until the chocolate sets completely, about 5 to 10 minutes. Slide an angled metal spatula under the medallions to release them from the paper. Can be stored in an airtight container at room temperature for about 2 weeks.

Makes about 18 medallions

Chocolate Caramel Pecan Patties

I always keep the ingredients for these candies on hand, so that I can whip up a batch at a moment's notice. They are quick, easy, and absolutely delicious, made with pecans, lots of milk chocolate, and Nestlé Bulk Caramel, a delectable, ready-made product that is sold by the 1- or 5-pound loaf in cake decorating and candy supply shops and through specialty mail-order catalogs. If you can't find it (keep looking!), substitute a comparable amount of packaged caramels from the supermarket, combined with 2 or 3 tablespoons of heavy cream. Make a smaller batch if you must, but you'll be sorry if you do.

❧ Placing walnut-sized mounds of caramel on bed of pecans.

1 pound pecan halves

1 ¼ pounds Nestlé Bulk Caramel

2 pounds milk chocolate, coarsely chopped, plus 8 ounces milk chocolate, in chunks (for tempering)

❧ Letting the chocolate roll off the tip of the spoon onto the caramel pecan patty.

1. Clear a 3-foot-wide area of work space. Line the inside of a 15-by-10-inch jelly roll pan with waxed paper. Fill it with the pecans, pushing them close together to form a thick bed covering about ¾ of the pan, leaving the rest of the pan empty. Line 2 large rimless baking sheets with waxed paper, securing it with tape. Have at hand 3 teaspoons, 2 of them coated with vegetable-oil cooking spray.

2. In a medium bowl, microwave the caramel on high (100 percent) power until most of it is soft, but not runny, about 1 minute. Or, soften the caramel in a bowl over a pan of hot water over low heat. Use the soft portion of the caramel first, rewarming the rest as needed.

3. Using the 2 oiled teaspoons, scoop out a walnut-sized mound of caramel and place it in the upper left-hand corner of the bed of pecans, scraping it off with the other spoon. Repeat to make 16 more mounds, spaced ¾ inch apart, covering the entire bed of pecans. The warmer the caramel, the more it will spread, so if it's a little runny, leave extra room between the mounds. Let sit until the caramel patties are cool enough to handle.

4. Lift the patties out of the pecans. Break off any portions of the pecans that extend beyond the edges of the caramel and place them on the baking sheets, spaced ¾ inch apart. Let cool completely, or the latent heat will break the temper and blemish the surface of the finished candy.

5. Meanwhile, push the remaining pecans close together again, this time forming a thick bed of pecans covering half the pan. If the caramel has hardened, warm it as directed, but for slightly less time. Repeat, each time working with an increasingly narrower bed of pecans, until all the caramel and/or pecans are used.

6. Melt and temper the chopped chocolate (see page 22). Holding the bowl close to the sheet of patties, and using the unoiled teaspoon, scoop out 1 rounded teaspoonful of chocolate, scraping the bottom of the spoon on the edge of the bowl. Let the chocolate roll off the tip of the spoon onto the patty. Immediately jiggle the surface with the tip of the spoon to smooth the surface and cover the caramel completely. Repeat until all the patties are coated. Refrigerate each sheet as you finish with it until the chocolate sets, about 5 to 10 minutes. Stir the bowl of chocolate occasionally as you work, scraping the sides to keep the cooler chocolate from solidifying on the walls. If the chocolate starts to thicken before you're finished, place it in a pan or a slightly larger bowl over hot water for a few seconds or microwave it on low (30 percent) power in 10- to 15-second increments, never letting the temperature exceed 88°F.

7. Store the patties in an airtight container at room temperature for about 2 weeks. If there is any leftover chocolate, refrigerate it on a sheet of waxed paper until set and store in an airtight container at room temperature for future use.

Makes about 4 dozen patties

VARIATIONS:

Cashew Patties: Substitute cashews for the pecans and proceed as directed in the main recipe.

Macadamia Patties: Substitute macadamias for the pecans and proceed as directed in the main recipe.

Spanish Peanut Patties: Substitute Spanish peanuts for the pecans and proceed as directed in the main recipe.

Semisweet or White Chocolate Patties: Substitute semisweet or white chocolate for the milk chocolate and proceed as directed in the main recipe.

chocolate truffles

Like most chocolate-lovers, I always reach for a truffle when I want an intense chocolate experience. Truffles are among the richest of all chocolate confections and are as revered as the legendary French fungi for which they were named. Some truffles are lumpy, irregularly shaped balls that resemble their namesake, with a thick coating of unsweetened cocoa powder that simulates the soil in which the fungi grows. Others are perfectly shaped balls, bathed in a coat of tempered chocolate that is often hidden beneath a layer of finely ground nuts, shredded toasted coconut, or delicate chocolate shavings.

Truffles are made of premium chocolate and fresh dairy cream (and/or butter), a luxurious combination of ingredients known as ganache. Ganache is famous for its versatility. Unlike baking recipes that must be followed precisely, ganache recipes welcome experimentation. By varying the proportion of chocolate to cream in a recipe, you can make a mixture that is fluid enough to pour over a cake (see page 144), thick enough to use as a filling or icing, or stiff enough to roll into balls to form truffles.

There are two basic types of truffle mixtures: firm (for rolling into balls) and soft (for filling chocolate shells). Firm truffle mixtures generally require twice as much chocolate as cream to make them stiff enough to roll into balls. Soft truffle mixtures contain nearly equal amounts of chocolate and cream, making them almost impossible to roll by hand. Instead, they are used as near-liquid fillings in molded chocolate shells (see page 50). Truffles with soft centers are the favorites of vast numbers of chocolate connoisseurs throughout the world.

Flavoring Ganache

Since chocolate is the primary source of flavor in a ganache recipe, it is very important to use a brand of chocolate that you enjoy eating. You can also enhance the taste of the chocolate by adding flavoring oils and liqueurs. For a richer taste and a smoother mouth feel, replace some of the cream in the recipe with equal amounts of butter or crème fraîche. For a lighter mixture, dilute the heavy cream with half-and-half, which is lower in butterfat.

To embellish the flavor even more, you can infuse the hot cream in a truffle recipe by steeping fresh mint leaves, tea leaves, citrus fruit peels, or split vanilla beans in it for at least 15 minutes. Strain the infused cream, then add more cream to equal the original amount before reheating and combining it with the chocolate.

Shelf Life of Truffles

Truffle centers will begin to shrink and get moldy after about 2 weeks if stored at a moderate 72°F room temperature, but they will last for about 1 month if refrigerated. They will last almost indefinitely in the freezer, provided you package them in an airtight container. To avoid condensation during thawing, leave them in their original container in the refrigerator overnight, then allow them to come to room temperature before exposing them to the air. Many confectioners extend the shelf life of truffles by replacing some of the cream with light corn syrup, honey, or butter.

❧ Classic Chocolate Truffles, page 34.

Classic Chocolate Truffles

If you are new to truffle making, this is a perfect recipe for you. The firm ganache is simple to make, stiff enough to roll into balls, and produces truffles that are soft inside, yet firm enough on the outside to make handling and dipping them easy—even when they are at room temperature (the ideal temperature for centers).

1 cup sifted unsweetened cocoa powder,
    or 1 ½ cups skinned toasted hazelnuts
    (see page 7), finely chopped,
    or 1 ½ cups shredded coconut, toasted
    (see page 7)

Firm Ganache
8 ounces bittersweet or semisweet couverture
    chocolate, coarsely chopped
½ cup heavy (whipping) cream

1. Clear a 3-foot-wide area of work surface. Line a large rimless baking sheet with waxed paper, securing it with tape. Fit a 12-inch pastry bag with a No. 1A decorating tip with a ½-inch round opening. Fill one or more small, shallow bowls with cocoa, hazelnuts, or coconut.

2. To make the firm ganache: In the bowl of a food processor, pulse the chopped chocolate on and off until the pieces are the size of small granules. If you don't have a food processor, use a heavy French chef's knife to chop the chocolate very finely (see Note).

3. In a small, heavy saucepan, heat the cream over low heat until bubbles form around the edges of the pan. Pour the cream into a large bowl and let cool for about 1 minute. Add the chocolate granules all at once, shaking the bowl gently to submerge them in the cream. When the pieces are soft, begin stirring with a rubber spatula until the ganache mixture is smooth and thoroughly blended. If any pieces remain unmelted, briefly place the bowl of ganache over a pan or a slightly larger bowl of hot water, stirring gently until they melt completely.

4. Cover loosely and refrigerate, stirring occasionally, until a dollop of ganache dropped from the tip of the spatula holds its shape, about 30 minutes to 1 hour. (Some couverture chocolates set faster than others.)

5. Spoon half the ganache into the pastry bag (see page 15). Holding the bag perpendicular to the surface of the baking sheet, with the tip elevated about 1 inch, squeeze hard, lifting the tip slightly to allow a buildup of ganache about ¾ inch in diameter. Stop squeezing the bag and pull it away in a quick, circular motion to break the flow. Repeat, making rows of mounds spaced 1 inch apart, until all the ganache has been used. Alternatively, use a melon baller or a No. 100 ice cream scooper dipped in cornstarch to scoop out the balls. Refrigerate until firm, about 30 minutes.

6. Roll each mound into a ball between your palms, then roll the ball into the cocoa, nuts, or coconut to cover it completely. Place the truffle in a fluted candy cup. Repeat until all the ganache is used. Serve at once, or store refrigerated in an airtight container for up to 1 month (see page 32).

Makes 30 to 35 truffles

VARIATIONS:

Milk Chocolate Truffles: Use 12 ounces milk chocolate and proceed as directed in the main recipe.

White Chocolate Truffles: Use 12 ounces white chocolate, ⅓ cup cream. Proceed as directed in the main recipe.

Rich and Creamy Dark Chocolate Truffles: Use ⅓ cup cream, and add 2 tablespoons soft unsalted butter to the warm ganache. Proceed as directed in the main recipe.

Liqueur-Flavored Truffles: Adding liqueur to a truffle recipe will soften the mixture unless you add a comparable amount of chocolate. For every ounce of liqueur (2 tablespoons) that you add to a dark chocolate recipe, add 1 ounce of chocolate. Add 2 extra ounces of chocolate per ounce of liqueur in milk and white chocolate truffle recipes.

Mocha Truffles: Use 9 ounces semisweet chocolate and 2 teaspoons instant espresso coffee granules dissolved in the hot cream. Add 2 tablespoons coffee liqueur to the ganache mixture and proceed as directed in the main recipe.

Chocolate Note

Since all chocolates vary, some ganache mixtures may set up more firmly than others. Unfortunately, it's difficult to gauge how firmly the mixture will set while you're making it. If you're not satisfied with the results the first time, you can adjust the proportions the next time you make it. If your centers were too firm, add less chocolate or more cream. If they were too soft, add more chocolate or less cream.

chocolate dipping

During my days on the chocolate-festival circuit, I witnessed some rather strange things being dipped in chocolate for the sake of entertainment: pickles, sardines, hot peppers, grasshoppers, and—I kid you not—cast members of the now-defunct *Miami Vice* television show. Silliness aside, there are some legitimate reasons for dipping fresh and sugar-glazed fruit, nuts, cookies, salty tidbits, and all kinds of candy centers in chocolate: Chocolate improves their taste, enhances their appearance, and increases their value. Below are some ideas for dipping. The guidelines (at right) will help you learn the proper skills, but it is practice that makes perfect.

Dried and Glacé (Sugar-Glazed or Candied) Fruit: Medjool and Deglet Noir dates, prunes, Australian apricots (the best kind), pineapples, peaches, pears, kiwis, figs, orange peels, and orange slices.

Fresh Fruit: Strawberries, pitted Bing cherries, grapes, orange and tangerine segments, sliced kiwis, and frozen bananas.

Nuts: Brazil nuts, hazelnuts, cashews, macadamias, and almonds.

Cookies: Shortbread, butter cookies, biscotti, mandelbrot, and sandwiched wafers.

Salty Snacks: Pretzels, potato chips, and tortilla chips.

Candy Centers: Gum drops, marshmallow eggs, caramels, ganache, marzipan, and fondant.

Always temper chocolate used for dipping. Tempered chocolate clings to centers, dries quickly, maintains its shine at room temperature, and doesn't melt in your fingers the minute you touch it. Untempered melted chocolate does just the opposite.

Use bars or slabs of couverture chocolate, rather than chocolate chips or baking bars from the supermarket, for dipping purposes. When it comes to dipping, the better the bar of chocolate, the more fluid the melt and the easier it is to use.

Always melt and temper more chocolate than you need. It takes twice as much chocolate to dip centers as it does to coat them, so you will usually recoup about half of the original amount. Eight ounces of melted chocolate is enough to cover 1 pound of truffles (about 30), but you need an extra 8 ounces in order to have a deep-enough pool in which to dip them.

Dip in a cool room, ideally between 65° and 68°F (or approximately 20° cooler than the chocolate), with good air circulation. Dipped wet centers that linger in a warm room for more than 5 minutes will dry dull and streaked, even though they were dipped in tempered chocolate.

Centers to be dipped should be at room temperature, not cold or frozen. A dipped cold center will expand as it warms to room temperature, causing the chocolate shell to crack and the filling to ooze out.

Dip centers that are firm, with smooth surfaces, so they won't stick to your fingers or to the dipping fork. Until you are more experienced, select dry, firm centers from the categories listed on the left.

Chocolate-Dipped Fruit and Cookies

Chocolate complements most fruit flavors. Select varieties with dry surfaces, or pat them dry with paper towels before using to avoid contaminating the chocolate with juice or excessive moisture during the dipping procedure. Leaving the hulls on strawberries makes it easier to dip the berries and inhibits juice leakage. Select firm, noncrumbly cookies like shortbread, biscotti, and sandwiched wafers for dipping into chocolate.

1 pound semisweet couverture chocolate, coarsely chopped, plus 4 ounces semisweet couverture chocolate, in chunks (for tempering)

1 pound glacé fruit, unhulled fresh strawberries, or shortbread cookies

bowl to keep the cooler chocolate from solidifying on the walls. If the chocolate starts to thicken before you're finished, place it in a pan or slightly larger bowl of hot water for a few seconds or microwave it on low (30 percent) power in 10- to 15-second increments. Serve fresh fruit the same day you dip it. You can store dipped glacé fruit and cookies in an airtight container at a moderate room temperature for up to 1 week.

Makes one pound fruit or cookies

Chocolate Note
The chocolate will probably have absorbed moisture or will contain crumbs from the dipping procedure, so it should not be saved for future melting use. Instead, use it to make chocolate bark or nut clusters (page 28).

1. Melt and temper the chopped chocolate (see page 22).

2. Clear a 3-foot-wide area of work space. Line a large rimless baking sheet with waxed paper, securing it with tape. Place the fruit or cookies to be dipped to your left, the bowl of tempered chocolate in the center (on a folded towel, doubled in the back so that it tilts forward), and the lined baking sheet to your right. If you're left-handed, reverse the placement order.

3. Hold the fruit or cookie by the edge (or the strawberry by the hull) and immerse it halfway into the chocolate. Lift the piece out of the chocolate and, holding it over the bowl, shake it gently to drain the excess. Lightly scrape the bottom of the dipped piece on the side of the bowl and place it on the baking sheet, scraped-side-down. Repeat until the fruit or cookies are used up. Refrigerate until the chocolate sets, about 5 minutes. Stir the chocolate occasionally as you work, scraping the sides of the

Marbleized Dipped Strawberries

These dipped strawberries offer a welcome contrast to the more familiar ones that we all know and love. The dipping process is entertaining, as you never can predict exactly what kind of marbleized design you will get when you plunge a strawberry into a striped pool of chocolate.

8 ounces semisweet couverture chocolate, coarsely chopped, plus 2 ounces semisweet couverture chocolate, in chunks (for tempering)

1 ½ pounds white chocolate couverture, coarsely chopped, plus 6 ounces white chocolate couverture, in chunks (for tempering)

2 pints unhulled fresh strawberries

1. Melt and temper both chopped chocolates (see page 22). When not in use, place the bowl of dark chocolate in a pan or a slightly larger bowl of warm (90°F) water, replenishing the warm water as necessary. Stir the bowl of chocolate occasionally as you work, scraping the sides of the bowl. Dry the bottom of the bowl each time you remove it from the water. Pour all the white chocolate into a 10-inch pie plate.

2. Clear a 3-foot-wide area of work space. Line a large rimless baking sheet with waxed paper, securing it with tape. Place the strawberries to be dipped to your left, the plate of white chocolate in the center (on a folded towel to protect it from the cool work surface), and the lined baking sheet to your right. If you're left-handed, reverse the placement order.

3. Using a rubber spatula, drizzle vertical lines of dark chocolate across the surface of the white chocolate.

4. Holding it by its hull, stand a strawberry upright in the pool of chocolate. Rock it forward and backward, pressing the front and back of the strawberry against the surface of the chocolate, forming 2 marbleized flower petals. Holding it by its hull over the pie plate, shake it gently to drain the excess and place it on the lined baking sheet. Periodically, add more vertical stripes of dark chocolate, dragging the spatula through the pool with vertical strokes to level the surface. Repeat, selecting a fresh area of the pool of chocolate to dip each berry into. Arrange the dipped strawberries on the baking sheet in rows, spaced 1 inch apart.

5. Refrigerate until the chocolate sets, about 5 minutes. Let sit, lightly covered, at room temperature and serve within a few hours.

Makes 32 to 35 strawberries

Chocolate Note
The chocolate will probably absorb moisture from the strawberries, so it should not be saved for future melting purposes.

🍓 Rocking the strawberry forward and backward in the pool of chocolate. (Inset)
🍓 Arranging the dipped fruit on a waxed paper–lined baking sheet.

Hand-Dipped Truffles

If you loved to finger paint as a child, you will enjoy hand-dipping centers in chocolate. These double-dipped truffles, also known as Zurich-style truffles, are identifiable by their spiked surface, the result of having been rolled, while wet, on a grid-type wire cake rack. When it comes to truffle making, "double-dipping" does not imply a social impropriety. The first coat protects the chocolate shell from tearing as it is being "roughed up" on the grid. The second coat seals the inevitable cracks that form when cold centers are dipped in chocolate (see page 36). This method is recommended for dipping soft truffle centers and centers that must be dipped cold.

Rolling the truffle center in your palm produces professional-looking results every time because it eliminates the buildup of excess chocolate that often identifies the work of an inexperienced candy maker. If possible, enlist the aid of another person to roll the truffle balls as you dip them, to speed the process and to make it more enjoyable. If you're squeamish about sticking your hand in melted chocolate (or if you have hot, sweaty hands), wear tight-fitting latex gloves (see page 13).

❧ Piping rows of ganache rounds.

❧ Rolling a truffle in tempered chocolate.

❧ Rolling a truffle on a grid rack.

Firm Ganache (page 34)

1 pound semisweet couverture chocolate,
    coarsely chopped, plus 4 ounces
    semisweet couverture chocolate,
    in chunks (for tempering)

1. Clear a 3-foot-wide area of work surface. Line 2 large rimless baking sheets with waxed paper, securing it with tape. Fit a 12-inch pastry bag with a No. 1A decorating tip with a ½-inch round opening. Have at hand a grid-type wire cake rack and a pair of latex gloves.

2. Prepare the firm ganache. Cool, pipe, and refrigerate the ganache mounds as directed.

3. Dust both hands and one of the baking sheets with cornstarch. Roll the mounds into balls between your palms, arranging them in rows on the baking sheet. Let sit at room temperature for several hours (or overnight) until a thin crust forms. Line the other baking sheet with fresh waxed paper.

4. When you're ready to dip, melt and temper the chopped chocolate (see page 22). Place the bowl in a pan or a slightly larger bowl of warm (90°F) water, replenishing the warm water as necessary. Stir the chocolate occasionally as you work, scraping the sides of the bowl. Place the firm balls to your left, the bowl of tempered chocolate in front of you, the freshly lined baking sheet to your right, and a grid-type wire cake rack next to it over a sheet of waxed paper. (If you're left-handed, reverse the order.)

5. Smear a small handful of chocolate on the palm of your left hand. Roll a truffle around in it with the fingertips of your right hand until it is completely covered with chocolate. (If you're left-handed, reverse the order.) Pick it up with your fingertips and place it back on the baking sheet. Repeat, coating your palm frequently with chocolate, until all of the truffles have been dipped. Let set at room temperature until the truffles peel off the paper easily.

6. Dip the truffles again, this time placing 5 or 6 of them at a time on the grid rack. While they are still wet, roll them around the rack to rough up their surface, placing them back on the baking sheet before they have time to set up on the rack. Refrigerate for about 5 minutes. Serve at once in fluted candy cups or refrigerate for up to 1 month.

7. Refrigerate the leftover chocolate on a sheet of waxed paper until set, and store in an airtight container at room temperature for future use.

Makes 30 to 35 truffles

FORK-DIPPING TRUFFLES

I used to dread dipping truffles with a fork. No matter what I did, they always stuck to the fork and looked awful by the time I finished. Now, after much trial and error, I have finally mastered the technique and I actually look forward to dipping truffles this way. Here are my hard-earned tips for trouble-free fork dipping:

Always dip *firm* centers, like the firm ganache on page 34. Soft centers will stick to the fork no matter what you do.

Dip centers that are at room temperature. Dipping cold or frozen centers in a bowl of chocolate is like putting ice cubes in a glass of water. They will cool it down quickly, causing the chocolate to thicken and become difficult to use.

Use a small, *shallow* bowl for dipping. If the bowl is too deep, you'll spend more time fishing for lost truffles than dipping them.

Select the right kind of fork. If you don't have a professional dipping fork (see page 13), use a regular dinner fork with long, narrow tines. Use the fork to maneuver the center and to stir the chocolate between dips. Wipe it periodically to keep it free of excess chocolate.

Set up the work area ahead of time. Place the centers to be dipped to your left, the bowl of tempered chocolate in the center (on a folded towel, doubled in the back so that the bowl tilts forward), and a large rimless baking sheet lined with waxed paper to your right. Reverse the order if you're left-handed.

Work quickly and systematically. Use one hand to drop the center into the bowl and the other to submerge it, lift it out, and transfer it to the waxed paper–lined baking sheet.

Once the wet center has been placed on the baking sheet, don't touch it until it sets. Jarring it will tear a little hole in the bottom. (If that happens, plug it with a dab of chocolate.)

Refrigerate the dipped centers promptly. If the room is warm, dip and refrigerate a dozen centers at a time.

❧ Hand-Dipped Truffles, page 40.

Fork-Dipped Truffles

Truffles can be dipped with either a wire-loop dipping fork or a tined dipping fork (see page 13). The loop fork, which is used for dipping round centers, produces truffles with a decorative swirl on top. For a smooth surface, use a tined fork. To add interesting textures to an assortment of truffles or to disguise imperfect ones, sprinkle them with finely ground hazelnuts, pistachios, dragées, or unsweetened cocoa powder while they are still wet. To decorate the tops of smooth, dry truffles, drizzle them with lines of a contrasting shade of chocolate.

Firm Ganache (page 34)

1 pound semisweet couverture chocolate, coarsely chopped, plus 4 ounces semisweet couverture chocolate, in chunks (for tempering)

Unsweetened cocoa powder for dusting, or ¼ cup skinned toasted hazelnuts or pistachios (see page 7), finely chopped

2 ounces milk chocolate, coarsely chopped, plus one ½-ounce chunk milk chocolate (for tempering)

1 tablespoon tiny dragées (optional)

1. Clear a 3-foot-wide area of work surface. Line 2 large rimless baking sheets with waxed paper, securing it with tape. Fit a 12-inch pastry bag with a No. 1A decorating tip with a ½-inch round opening.

2. Prepare the firm ganache. Cool, pipe, and refrigerate the ganache mounds as directed.

3. Dust both hands and a baking sheet with cornstarch. Roll the mounds into balls between your palms, arranging them in rows on the baking sheet. Let sit at room temperature for several hours (or overnight) until a thin crust forms. Line the other baking sheet with fresh waxed paper. When you're ready to dip, melt and temper the chopped couverture chocolate (see page 16). Place the centers to be dipped to your left, the bowl of chocolate in the center (on a folded towel, doubled in the back so that the bowl tilts forward), and the freshly lined baking sheet to your right. Reverse the order if you're left-handed.

4. To dip truffles with a wire-loop fork: Stir the chocolate with the dipping fork in the place where you will be dropping the truffle. With your other hand, drop the truffle there, rounded-side-down. Push the truffle under the surface with the fork. Lift it out, supported underneath by the fork. Tap the bottom of the fork very lightly on the surface of the pool of chocolate several times, draining the excess chocolate from the truffle. Move the truffle to the baking sheet. With your hand close to the paper, give your wrist a quick turn to drop the truffle onto the paper, rounded-side-up. Lightly touch the top of the truffle with the wire loop to mark it with a decorative swirl. Stir the bowl of chocolate occasionally as you work, scraping the sides to keep the cooler chocolate from solidifying on the walls. If the chocolate starts to thicken before you're finished, place it in a pan or a slightly larger bowl of hot water for a few seconds or microwave it on low (30 percent) power in 12- to 15-second increments, never letting the temperature exceed 90°F.

5. To dip truffles with a tined fork: Immerse the truffle, rounded-side-up, pushing it under the surface with the fork. Lift it out, partially supported underneath by the fork, but with a little of the truffle extended beyond the tines. Tap the bottom of the fork very lightly on the surface of the pool of chocolate several times, draining the excess chocolate from the truffle. Lightly scrape the fork on the edge of the bowl as you move toward the baking sheet. With the truffle as close to the paper as possible

❧ Fancy Forked-Dipped Truffles.

and the tines of the fork angled up slightly, set the extended edge of the truffle down first, followed by the rest. Stir the bowl of chocolate occasionally as you work, scraping the sides of the bowl. Warm over hot water, if needed, as directed in Step 4.

6. To decorate the tops with cocoa or nuts: Sprinkle a light dusting of cocoa over the wet truffles with a sieve held several inches above the baking sheet. Or, sprinkle them with nuts by hand. Refrigerate until set, about 5 minutes.

7. To decorate the tops with piped lines of chocolate: Melt and temper the chopped milk chocolate (see page 16). Spoon it into a parchment decorating bag, cutting a ⅛-inch opening in the tip. Hold the bag about 8 inches above the surface of the dry truffles. Using sweeping side-to-side movements, pipe a pattern of horizontal lines across the tops of the truffles. Sprinkle the wet lines with the dragées, if you like. Refrigerate until set, about 5 minutes. Serve at once in fluted candy cups, or refrigerate for up to 1 month.

8. Refrigerate the leftover chocolate on a sheet of waxed paper until set and store in an airtight container at room temperature for future use.

Makes 30 to 35 truffles

Mouse Truffles

Everyone always looks twice when they spot these little fellows sitting on a dessert plate—especially when they're accompanied with a slice of white chocolate "Swiss cheese" (see page 111). The ganache bodies are formed with a pastry bag using a simple piping technique known as "beading" (see page 75), but you can also form them by hand (see Note). Since these truffles are an odd shape, I like to bottom-coat them with a thin layer of chocolate before I dip them, which makes them easier to handle.

30 to 35 pieces Chocolate Spaghetti Twigs
    (page 89), cut into 2-inch segments,
    or black shoestring licorice, sliced length
    wise and cut into 2-inch segments

Firm Ganache (page 34)

¼ cup sliced almonds, toasted (see page 7)
    and cut crosswise into ½-inch-long pieces

1 pound semisweet couverture chocolate,
    coarsely chopped, plus 4 ounces semisweet
    couverture chocolate, in chunks (for
    tempering)

1 ounce white chocolate, coarsely chopped

1 ounce milk chocolate, coarsely chopped

1. At least 3 hours ahead, prepare the chocolate spaghetti twigs. Prepare the firm ganache and cool as directed.

2. Clear a 3-foot-wide area of smooth work surface. Line 3 large rimless baking sheets with waxed paper, securing it with tape. Stack one of the lined sheets on top of another one. Fit a 12-inch pastry bag with a No. 1A decorating tip with a ½-inch round opening. Arrange 35 pairs of the almond slices on a sheet of waxed paper. Have at hand a 3- or 4-tined dipping fork, several toothpicks, and an angled metal spatula.

3. Spoon half the ganache into the pastry bag. Hold the bag at a 30-degree angle to the top edge of the lined baking sheet, with the tip barely touching it. Squeeze the bag, allowing the force of the ganache to lift the tip off the surface. Maintaining a steady pressure on the bag, hold that position long enough for the ganache to swell and fan out to about ¾ inch. Relax the pressure on the bag as you lower the tip to the surface, tapering the ganache to a point (the mouse's nose). The body should be ¾ inch wide and 2 inches long. Repeat, piping more mounds (about 30 to 35 total), spacing them 1 inch apart, replenishing the bag with more ganache until all of it is used.

4. Push the cut ends of 2 almond-slice "ears" into the mounds of ganache about ½ inch back from the tip of the "nose." Refrigerate until firm, 30 minutes to 1 hour.

5. Melt and temper the chopped semisweet chocolate (see page 22). Place the truffles to be dipped to your left, the bowl of chocolate in the center (on a folded towel, doubled in the back so that the bowl tilts forward) and the 2 stacked baking sheets to your right. Reverse the order if you're left-handed. Using a metal spatula, apply a thin layer of melted chocolate to the bottom of each truffle. Arrange them in rows on the clean baking sheet and let set at room temperature, about 5 minutes. Reverse the placement of the 2 baking sheets, relining the first one with fresh paper.

6. Dip the truffle in the chocolate, rounded-side-up, pushing it under the surface with the dipping fork and scooping chocolate over it. Lift it out, partially supported underneath by the fork, but with a little of the truffle extended beyond the tines. Tap the bottom of the fork very lightly on the surface of the chocolate several times to drain the excess chocolate. Lightly scrape the fork on the edge of the bowl as you move the truffle toward the baking sheet. With the truffle as close to the paper as possible and the tines angled up slightly, set the extended edge of the truffle down first, followed by the rest. Repeat until all

the truffles have been dipped, using the third baking sheet if necessary. Refrigerate until set, about 5 minutes. Stir the bowl of chocolate occasionally as you work, scraping the sides to keep the cooler chocolate from solidifying on the walls. If the chocolate starts to thicken before you're finished, place it in a pan or a slightly larger bowl of hot water for a few seconds or microwave it on low (30 percent) power in 12- to 15-second increments, never letting the temperature exceed 90°F.

7. Jab a mouse with a toothpick to make a hole for the tail. Dip the end of one piece of chocolate spaghetti into the leftover chocolate and insert it into the hole. Repeat with the remaining mice.

8. Melt the white chocolate. Pour it directly onto the work surface and turn it with an angled metal spatula until it feels cool (see page 24). Using a toothpick, apply 2 white dots on the mouse's face for the eyes. Melt and cool the milk chocolate in the same way. When the white dots are dry, dot them with milk chocolate, adding another dot for the nose. Serve at once, or cover and refrigerate for up to 1 month.

9. Refrigerate the leftover chocolate on a sheet of waxed paper until set and store in an airtight container at room temperature for future use.

Makes 30 to 35 truffles

Chocolate Note
To form the mouse bodies by hand, use a cornstarch-dusted small ice cream scooper (see page 14), scoop out 30 to 35 mounds of ganache, and place them on a waxed paper–lined baking sheet. Roll between cornstarch-coated palms to form bodies that are ¾ inch wide and 2 inches long. Proceed as directed for the piped bodies.

Chocolate Swan Truffles

These chocolate swans can be served as a confection or as a dessert in a pool of chocolate sauce. The procedure for making them consists of several steps, each of which can be done at a different time. To make things easier, pipe the wings and necks a few days or weeks in advance and the truffle centers closer to the time you will need them. When it's time to dip the truffles and assemble all the pieces, you'll then be able to focus all your attention on that task.

The necks and wings are piped over patterns like the ones provided (see pattern No. 1). Piping over a pattern with chocolate is a lot like using a crayon in a coloring book, but in this case it's okay to go outside the lines. The purpose of these patterns is to guide you, not to impose restrictions on you.

Swan and mouse truffles have the same body shape, but in reverse: The mouse's nose is the swan's tail. Both are made the same way: either with a pastry bag or shaped by hand (see page 47). Bottom-coating the bodies with chocolate makes it much easier to dip them.

> Firm Ganache for White Chocolate Truffles
>   (page 35)
>
> 1 ½ pounds white couverture chocolate, coarsely chopped, plus 6 ounces white couverture chocolate, in chunks (for tempering)

1. Clear a 3-foot-wide area of work surface. Have at hand three 8 ½-by-11-inch sheets of paper and 3 pattern boards with waxed-paper liners (see page 15). Using the patterns that are provided, trace 20 necks on one sheet and the left- and right-side wings on the others. Slide the sheets under the waxed-paper liners of the pattern boards. Have at hand 2 parchment decorating bags (see page 10), a toothpick, an angled metal spatula, and a small stick the diameter of a pencil.

2. Melt 8 ounces of the chopped chocolate, tempering it with a 2-ounce chunk (see page 22). Place the bowl of chocolate in a pan or in a slightly larger bowl of 88° F water, replenishing the warm water as necessary. Stir the chocolate occasionally as you work, scraping the sides of the bowl to keep the cooler chocolate from solidifying on the walls. Spoon some of the chocolate into a parchment bag, filling it half full. Cut a ⅜-inch opening in the tip.

3. To pipe the necks: Elevate the tip slightly above the neck pattern, squeezing the bag with steady but gentle pressure to allow a small bulb to form for the head before piping the rest of the neck. Pull out a beak with a toothpick. Repeat to pipe 19 other necks. Refrigerate until set, about 10 minutes. Slide the spatula under the necks, turning them over gently. Pipe the backs of the necks. Refrigerate for about 5 minutes.

4. To pipe the wings: Fill another parchment bag half full of chocolate. Cut a ⅜-inch opening in the tip of the bag. Lightly touch the wing pattern at the point where the feathers meet. Using side-to-side movements, pipe 4 or 5 thick lines, emulating feathers. Repeat to pipe a total of 20 pairs of wings. Refrigerate until set, about 10 minutes. Refrigerate the leftover chocolate on a sheet of waxed paper until set.

5. Prepare the white chocolate firm ganache, cooling it as directed.

6. Fit a 12-inch pastry bag with a No. 1A decorating tip with a ½-inch round opening. Line the 2 large rimless baking sheets with waxed paper, securing it with tape. Have at hand an angled metal spatula and a 3- or 4-tined dipping fork.

7. Spoon half the ganache into the pastry bag. Pipe a 2 ¼-inch-long-by-1-inch-wide teardrop-shaped mound on a baking sheet (see page 46). Repeat to pipe 19 more mounds, spacing them 1 inch apart, replenishing the bag with more ganache until all of it is used. Using a small stick or the side of your finger, indent the front of each swan, forming a ¼-inch vertical niche for the neck. Refrigerate until firm, 30 minutes to 1 hour.

8. Melt and temper the rest of the chopped chocolate. Place the truffles to be dipped to your left, the bowl of chocolate in the center (on a folded towel, doubled in the back so that the bowl tilts forward), and the other baking sheet to your right, with the necks and wings (arranged in pairs) nearby. (Reverse the order if you're left-handed.) Using a metal spatula, apply a thin layer of chocolate to the bottom of each truffle. Arrange them in rows on the clean baking sheet and let set at room temperature, about 5 minutes. Reverse the placement of the 2 baking sheets, relining the first one with fresh waxed paper.

9. Dip 2 or 3 successive truffles in the chocolate at a time (see page 46), alternately attaching the wings and necks to them before the chocolate dries. Dab the neck with a little chocolate at its point of contact with the truffle to help secure it. If the chocolate starts to thicken before you're finished, place it in a pan or a slightly larger bowl of hot water for a few seconds or microwave it on low (30 percent) power in 10- to 15-second increments, never letting the temperature exceed 88°F. Refrigerate the truffles until set, about 10 minutes. Serve at once or refrigerate for up to 1 month.

10. Refrigerate the leftover chocolate on a sheet of waxed paper until set and store in an airtight container at room temperature for future use.

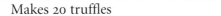

Makes 20 truffles

❧ The necks and wings are piped over 3 pattern sheets. Using 8½-by-11-inch paper, pipe 20 necks on the first sheet, the left-side wing on the second, and the right-side wing on the third.

Death by Truffles

Here is a truffle to die for! One bite and you will know why truffles with soft centers are in a class of their own. To save time and aggravation, you should have enough molds to fill about 48 cavities at one time. It takes a lot of chocolate to mold the shells, but you will recoup most of it before you're finished.

2 pounds bittersweet couverture chocolate, coarsely chopped, plus 8 ounces bittersweet couverture chocolate, in chunks (for tempering)

Soft Ganache
6 ounces bittersweet chocolate, coarsely chopped
½ cup heavy (whipping) cream
2 tablespoons (¼ stick) unsalted butter, at room temperature
1 tablespoon framboise or other liqueur

1. Clear a 3-foot-wide area of work surface and line it with waxed paper. Have at hand 4 flat molds with about 12 deep cavities per sheet, a teaspoon, a wall scraper with a 6-inch blade, a grid-type wire cake rack over a sheet of waxed paper, and about 4 parchment decorating bags (see page 10).

2. Melt and temper the chopped chocolate (see page 22). When not in use, place the bowl in a pan or a slightly larger bowl of warm (90°F) water, replenishing the warm water as necessary. Stir the bowl of chocolate occasionally, scraping the sides to keep the cooler chocolate from solidifying on the walls. Dry the bottom of the bowl each time you remove it from the water. Mold about 48 chocolate shells in the flat molds (see page 61), leaving them in the molds. Refrigerate the surplus and leftover chocolate on waxed paper until set, 5 to 10 minutes. Set aside at room temperature.

3. To make the soft ganache: In the bowl of a food processor, pulse the chopped chocolate on and off until the pieces are the size of small granules. If you don't have a food processor, use a heavy French chef's knife to chop the chocolate very finely. In a small, heavy saucepan, heat the cream over low heat until bubbles form around the edges of the pan. Pour the cream into a large bowl and let cool for about 1 minute. Add the chocolate granules all at once, shaking the bowl gently to submerge them in the cream. When the pieces are soft, begin stirring with a rubber spatula until the ganache mixture is smooth and thoroughly blended. If any pieces remain unmelted, briefly place the bowl of ganache in a bowl of hot water, stirring gently until they melt completely. Stir in the butter in 2 additions, incorporating one before adding the next. Stir in the liqueur. Let cool at room temperature to no warmer than 90°F.

4. To fill the molded shells with ganache: Spoon about ½-cup filling into a parchment decorating bag, cutting a ¼-inch opening in the tip. Insert the tip deep into the shell, squeezing the bag until the filling reaches to within ⅛ inch of the top. Release pressure and pull the tip away sideways to avoid leaving a point on the surface. Using another parchment bag, repeat until all the filling is used. Let sit at room temperature for at least 30 minutes.

5. To seal the cavities: Remelt and retemper the leftover chocolate. Using a spoon, fill a parchment bag half full of chocolate. Cut a ¼-inch opening in the tip. Pipe the chocolate over the filling, extending it slightly over the rim. Repeat to seal all of the cavities. Tap the back of the molds on the work surface. Using the wall scraper, scrape the surplus chocolate off the tops of the molds back into the bowl of chocolate. Refrigerate the molds until set, about 5 to 10 minutes. Refrigerate the leftover chocolate on a sheet of waxed paper until set; store in an airtight container at room temperature for future use. Line the work surface with waxed paper.

6. To release the chocolate from the mold: Tap the back of the mold once on the work surface. Turn it over onto the waxed paper; the pieces should drop out easily. If they don't, flex the mold. Repeat to release the chocolate in the other molds. Place the truffles in fluted candy cups and serve at once, or refrigerate in an airtight container for up to 1 month.

| Makes about 48 truffles |

Peanut Butter Meltaways

While truffles are made of chocolate and cream, meltaways contain coconut butter or nut paste (usually almond or hazelnut). These fats soften the texture of the chocolate, giving the mixture a wonderful melt-in-the-mouth quality. Randy Hofberger, the technical manager of customer services at Nestlé Chocolate and Confections Company in Burlington, Wisconsin, developed this excellent meltaway candy recipe using their Natural Peanut-Flavored Icecap Caps, a popular confectionery coating product that comes in a handy morsel-shaped form for easy melting. The mixture, which is soft and creamy, is a delicious filling to use inside molded milk chocolate shells.

> 2 pounds milk chocolate, coarsely chopped, plus 8 ounces milk chocolate, in chunks (for tempering)
>
> **Peanut Butter Filling**
> 6 ounces Nestlé Natural Peanut-Flavored Icecap Caps
>
> ½ cup creamy peanut butter
>
> Pinch of salt

1. Clear a 3-foot-wide area of work surface and line it with waxed paper. Have at hand 4 flat molds with 12 deep cavities, a teaspoon, a wall scraper with a 6-inch blade, a grid-type wire cake rack over a sheet of waxed paper, and about 4 parchment decorating bags (see page 10).

2. Melt and temper the chopped milk chocolate (see page 22). When not in use, place the bowl of chocolate in a pan or a slightly larger bowl of warm (88°F) water, replenishing the warm water as necessary. Stir the chocolate occasionally, scraping the sides of the bowl to keep the cooler chocolate from solidifying on the walls. Dry the bottom of the bowl each time you remove it from the water. Mold about 48 chocolate shells in the flat molds (see page 61), leaving them in the molds. Refrigerate the surplus and leftover chocolate on waxed paper until set, 5 to 10 minutes. Set aside until later.

3. To make the filling: Place half the Nestlé Icecap Caps in a bowl positioned over a slightly larger bowl of hot (130° to 140°F) water. Let the Caps begin to melt before stirring with a rubber spatula. Add the rest of the Caps gradually, allowing each addition to melt before adding the next. Add the peanut butter and salt, stirring until completely blended in. Let cool at room temperature to about 88°F.

4. To fill the molded shells: Spoon half the filling into a parchment bag. Cut a ¼-inch opening in the tip. Insert the tip deep into the shell, squeezing the bag until the filling reaches to within ⅛ inch of the top. Release pressure and pull the tip away sideways to avoid leaving a point on the surface. Fill another parchment bag and repeat until the filling is used up. Let sit at room temperature for at least 30 minutes.

5. To seal the cavities: Remelt and retemper the leftover chocolate. Using a spoon, fill a parchment bag half full of chocolate. Cut a ¼-inch opening in the tip. Pipe the chocolate over the filling, extending it slightly over the rim. Repeat to seal all the cavities. Tap the bottom of the molds on the work surface. Using the wall scraper, scrape the surplus chocolate off the top of the molds back into the bowl of chocolate. Refrigerate the molds until set, about 5 to 10 minutes. Refrigerate the leftover chocolate on a sheet of waxed paper until set; store in an airtight container at room temperature for future use. Line the work surface with waxed paper.

6. To release the chocolates from the mold: Tap the bottom of the mold once on the work surface. Turn it over onto the waxed paper; the pieces should drop out easily. If they don't, flex the mold. Repeat to release the chocolate in the other molds. Place the meltaways in fluted candy cups and serve at once, or store in an airtight container at a cool (65°F) room temperature for 6 to 9 months.

Makes about 48 meltaways

❧ Chocolate–Butter Pecan Toffee, page 54.

Chocolate—Butter Pecan Toffee

No candy repertoire is complete without a recipe for butter-rich, chocolate-dipped, pecan-encrusted toffee. This one is tender and full of the buttery flavor that most people find absolutely irresistible.

Ideally, you should have an 18-by-24-inch marble slab to make this toffee, but an 18-by-12-inch heavyweight baking sheet will work, too. Perhaps this recipe will give you the incentive to invest in a piece of marble—the bigger the better—so that you can double and quadruple the amount you make each time.

To simplify things, I've omitted the tempering step, since the chocolate is not visible once it's coated with chopped nuts. If you omit the nuts, the chocolate must be tempered. It is helpful, but not essential, to have a friend roll the toffee pieces in the nuts for you while you do the dipping. It will be easier to convince that person to help once he or she has tasted the final product.

1 ½ pounds pecans, coarsely chopped

1 cup (2 sticks) butter, cut into chunks

⅓ cup hot water

1 ¼ cups sugar

1 pound milk chocolate, coarsely chopped

❧ Laying the toffee on the chocolate to coat it.

❧ Scraping the excess chocolate off the toffee.

❧ Sprinkling the coated toffee with nuts.

1. Grease an 18-by-24-inch marble slab or a heavy 18-by-12-inch baking sheet and a long, angled metal spatula with vegetable oil. If you're using a baking sheet, place it on a wire cake rack on top of several thicknesses of newspaper to protect the work surface. Have at hand a candy thermometer, a long wooden spoon, 2 hot pads, 2 large baking sheets lined with waxed paper, 2 extra sheets of waxed paper, an unlined sided baking sheet, a 10-inch pie plate, and a pair of latex gloves.

2. Test the accuracy of the candy thermometer (see page 12), leaving it in the hot water until needed. Pour the pecans onto the unlined baking sheet.

3. In a heavy 3-quart pan, combine the butter and hot water. Cook over medium heat until the butter melts and the mixture comes to a boil. Add the sugar in a steady stream and cook, stirring constantly, until the sugar dissolves and the mixture returns to a boil. Attach the thermometer to the side of the pan.

4. Raise the heat to medium high and continue to cook, stirring constantly, until the temperature reaches 300°F, about 10 minutes. At first, the mixture will appear foamy and pale yellow in color. As it approaches 260°F, it will thicken and begin to pull away from the sides of the pan. Keep stirring. At 280°F, the color will change from pale yellow to tan. It will continue to darken as it reaches 300°F. Turn off the heat. Remove the thermometer and soak it in the pan of hot water with the wooden spoon. If the fat should suddenly separate and float to the top as you're cooking the toffee, add 1 or 2 tablespoons of sugar and continue cooking it to 320°F, stirring vigorously until it becomes homogenous again.

5. Holding the hot pan close to the marble or baking sheet, pour the mixture into an oblong pool without scraping the pan. Be careful; it is dangerously hot. Using the long metal spatula, spread the mixture thinly across most of the marble or the baking sheet. (Tilting the baking sheet helps to spread it.) Immediately slide the spatula under the toffee to release it from the marble. The toffee will set and be cool enough to handle within 5 minutes on the marble and within 10 minutes on the baking sheet. Break it into irregular-sized pieces, stacking layers of them between sheets of waxed paper on one of the baking sheets.

6. To coat the toffee with chocolate and nuts: Clear a 3-foot-wide area of work surface. Place the toffee pieces to your left, the pie plate in the center with a lined baking sheet behind it, and the pecans to your right. Reverse the order if you're left-handed.

7. Melt the chocolate (see page 16). Pour all of it into the pie plate. With gloved hands, pick up the first piece of toffee with your left hand and lay it on the chocolate. Coat both sides with your right (dipping) hand. Reverse hands if you're left-handed. Hold the edge of the dipped piece with the fingertips of your clean hand while the thumb and index finger of your dipping hand scrape off the excess chocolate. Place it in the bed of pecans along with the next 4 dipped pieces. Using your clean other hand, pick up a handful of nuts and sprinkle them over the wet pieces, coating them completely. Turn them over, sprinkle them with more nuts, and place them on the baking sheet behind the pie plate. Repeat, dipping and coating 5 pieces at a time, and stacking them directly on top of one another on the baking sheet. Refrigerate them until the chocolate sets, about 20 minutes. Store in an airtight container at room temperature for up to 1 month—under lock and key.

Makes about 2½ pounds toffee

chocolate magic tricks

This chapter is filled with all the little tricks that make working with chocolate so much fun. If you are too timid to do some of these things with real chocolate, by all means use confectionery coating (see page 4). Confectionery coating is an excellent medium for learning to work artistically with chocolate because it does not require tempering. I began using Nestlé Icecap coatings over twenty years ago, and I still use them today for many decorative purposes.

Whether you work in chocolate or confectionery coating, don't be intimidated by the length of any of the instructions. Many of them take longer to read than to *do*.

molding chocolate

My enthusiasm for molding has not diminished since I accidentally discovered years ago that I could mold chocolate place cards and lollipops in metal cookie cutters, chocolate platters in pizza pans, and chocolate candy boxes in cake pans. My collection of unconventional molds now includes baking sheets, tart shells, muffin tins, mixing bowls, disposable cups, trays and platters of every shape and size, plastic containers from take-out restaurants, empty plastic ice cream tubs, plastic inserts from packaged cookies, and other equally bizarre receptacles.

My collection also includes hundreds of commercially made plastic molds, all of which are made of FDA-approved food-safe polycarbonate plastic. Plastic molds have many advantages over the antique metal ones that are also in my collection. They are less expensive, they cool down faster, and they return to room temperature more quickly, all of which makes them ideal choices for molding chocolate. Most plastic molds are transparent, which allows you to peek inside to see if they contain air bubbles and to know, by observing their frosted appearance, when the chocolate has pulled away from the sides of the mold enough to be unmolded. Cake decorating and candy supply shops sell a wide variety of inexpensive plastic molds in many shapes and forms.

Molding chocolate is a magical experience no matter how many times you do it.

These simple guidelines will show you how much fun it can be, too:

Chocolate mirrors the surface it touches. Select metal or food-grade plastic molds with shiny, scratch-free molding surfaces, unless a design is engraved or embossed on the surface (which makes them all the more appealing).

Molds should be clean, dry, and at room temperature (68° to 72°F). Buff the cavities with a soft cloth before using.

If the mold has a plastic ridge around the edge, cut it off with sharp scissors so that the surface surrounding the open cavities is flat.

Always mold with tempered chocolate. It sets up quickly, pulls away from the sides of the mold when it dries, and releases easily. Untempered chocolate does just the opposite.

Deposit chocolate on the *inside* of a mold unless the mold is deflatable, such as a balloon. If you spread or paint it on the outside of a mold, it will grip the walls tightly and won't let go.

Tap the bottom of a filled mold on the work surface to settle the chocolate and to release the air bubbles.

Mold chocolate in a warm room, but chill the filled molds in a cool (45° to 65°F) room or in the refrigerator (never in the freezer). Chill confectionery coating in the freezer only briefly.

To estimate how much chocolate you will need for any molding project, consider these factors: How many cavities are in each mold? What is their capacity? How many pieces do I need to mold? Do I have duplicate molds, or do I have to wait for one filled mold to set before I can reuse it? What is the temperature of the room? Do I have enough patience to try to keep a small amount of chocolate in temper while I wait for that mold to be ready to refill? If in doubt, always melt more than you need.

To release poorly tempered chocolate from a mold, refrigerate the mold for several hours, then turn it upside down and bang it on the work surface. Use leftover untempered chocolate for baking and candy recipes. For dipping, molding, and piping, melt it to 110° to 115°F and then retemper it (see page 22).

USING FLAT MOLDS

Conventional flat molds make chocolates with a flat back and a dimensional upper surface. One sheet usually contains duplicates of one design or a combination of several different ones. The cavities vary in size, depth, and capacity. My favorites tend to be generic in design: shells, leaves, hearts, faceted diamonds, rounds, squares, and ovals. Baking sheets, pizza pans, metal and plastic trays, lids, cake pans, and other similar food-safe receptacles make great flat molds, too.

Chocolate Patties

Ideally, you should have multiples of molds to speed the process and to alleviate the problem of keeping the chocolate in temper. To make 60 round 1-inch-diameter patties like these, you should have 3 molds containing 20 cavities each. Metal mini-muffin pans can be used to mold identical patties. This molding procedure is simple: fill, tap, refrigerate, invert, and release.

1 pound semisweet chocolate, coarsely chopped, plus 4 ounces semisweet chocolate, in chunks (for tempering)

1. Clear a 3-foot-wide area of work surface and line it with a sheet of waxed paper. Have at hand an infant's feeding spoon, an iced-tea spoon or a regular teaspoon, a 6-inch wall scraper, and 3 flat patty molds with 20 cavities per sheet.

2. Melt and temper the chopped chocolate (see page 22). Place the bowl on a folded cloth to protect it from the cool work surface. Stir it occasionally as you work, scraping the sides of the bowl.

3. Holding the mold near the bowl, spoon the chocolate into the cavities almost to the rim. Tap the bottom of the filled mold on the work surface several times. Push the wall scraper across the surface of the mold, allowing the excess to fall back into the bowl. Stir the chocolate before filling each of the remaining molds. To fill the cavities with a chocolate-filled parchment decorating bag, cut a ¼-inch opening in the tip. Hold the bag at a 90-degree angle to the center of each cavity, squeezing hard until the chocolate reaches the rim.

4. Refrigerate the molds until the bottoms appear frosted, about 15 minutes. Invert them over the waxed paper–lined work surface. Gently flex the sides or tap them on the back to release the chocolate. If the chocolate doesn't release, refrigerate it briefly and try again. Store the patties between layers of waxed paper in an airtight container at room temperature.

5. Refrigerate any leftover chocolate on a sheet of waxed paper until set and store in an airtight container at room temperature for future use.

Makes about sixty 1-inch patties

A Chocolate Plate

Chocolate cakes, pastries, and candies look absolutely spectacular when served on a chocolate plate. For special occasions, use an engraved silver tray to make a picture-perfect chocolate replica, complete with an identical engraved design. The larger the diameter of the mold, the thicker the plate should be and the more chocolate you will need.

1 ½ pounds white chocolate, coarsely chopped, plus 6 ounces white chocolate, in chunks (for tempering)

1. Place a sheet of waxed paper on the work surface. Melt and temper the chopped white chocolate (see page 22). Have at hand an angled metal spatula, a 10-inch round corrugated cake circle, and a 12-inch round metal or plastic tray.

2. Reserve 2 tablespoons of chocolate in a small cup (at room temperature) and pour the rest into the bottom of the tray mold, leveling and smoothing it with the angled spatula. Tap the bottom of the mold on the work surface several times. Refrigerate until the chocolate sets and the center feels cold, about 20 to 25 minutes.

3. To release the chocolate, grasp the mold with both hands, with your fingers touching the chocolate and your thumbs pressed against the back of the mold. Invert the mold over the paper-lined work surface, pressing the back gently to release the chocolate. If it doesn't release easily, refrigerate the mold briefly and try again.

4. Place the reserved cup of chocolate in a shallow bowl of warm water until it softens. Smear it in the center of the cake circle and attach the back of the chocolate plate to it to facilitate handling and to protect the tablecloth from chocolate smudges.

Makes one 12-inch round plate

USING HOLLOW MOLDS

One-piece metal and plastic molds with deep cavities can be used for making chocolate shells or thick dimensional pieces with flat backs. My favorite molds in this category, however, are stainless-steel bowls, cake pans, and disposable plastic cups, which I use to make edible chocolate serving containers. Two-piece hollow molds, which clamp together when filled with chocolate, are used to make hollow or solid three-dimensional figures such as bunnies, Santas, and other novelties.

❧ Spooning the chocolate into the cavities.

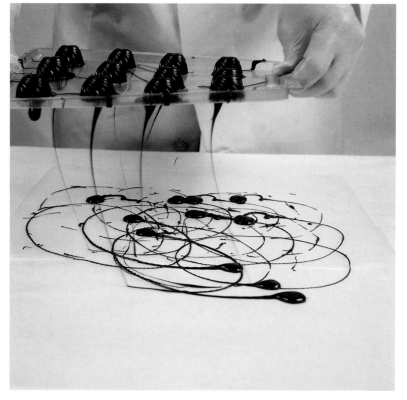

❧ Shaking the mold in a circular motion to drain surplus chocolate.

Chocolate Shells

Some molds have cavities deep enough to mold thin chocolate shells for making European-style filled chocolate confections (see page 50). Thin shells of cocoa butter–rich couverture offer no resistance when you bite into them and are certainly the most desirable, so if you're ever going to splurge when buying chocolate, this is the time to do it. The first molding step necessarily requires a lot of chocolate, but most of it is recoupable.

2 pounds semisweet couverture chocolate, coarsely chopped, plus 8 ounces semisweet couverture chocolate, in chunks (for tempering)

1. Clear a 3-foot-wide area of work surface and line it with waxed paper. Have at hand a teaspoon, a wire cake rack over a sheet of waxed paper, a 6-inch wall scraper, 2 or 3 parchment decorating bags (see page 10), and 4 flat molds with 12 deep cavities per sheet.

2. Melt and temper the chopped chocolate (see page 22). When not in use, place the bowl in a pan or a slightly larger bowl of warm (90°F) water, replenishing it with more warm water as needed. Stir the chocolate occasionally, scraping the sides of the bowl.

3. Holding the mold close to the bowl, spoon the chocolate into the cavities up to the rim. Tap the back of the mold on the work surface several times. Let sit while you fill the second mold.

4. Using both hands, invert the first mold over the covered work surface. Shake it in a circular motion to coax most of the surplus chocolate to run out, leaving the walls evenly coated. Drain the mold upside down on the wire cake rack while filling the second mold. Using the wall scraper, scrape the excess chocolate off the top of the first mold while draining the second. Refrigerate both molds until set, about 10 minutes.

5. Meanwhile, fill the other 2 molds with chocolate. Tap, shake, drain, scrape, and refrigerate them until set. Refrigerate the surplus and leftover chocolate on waxed paper until set, reserving it at room temperature until later.

6. To fill the molded shells: Proceed as directed (see page 50). To assure a proper seal, the filling must not reach the top of the chocolate shell. Flatten any peaks that form before sealing with chocolate.

7. To seal the cavities: Remelt and retemper the leftover chocolate. Using a spoon, fill a parchment bag half full of chocolate and cut a ¼-inch opening in the tip. Pipe the chocolate over the filling, extending it slightly over the rim. Repeat to seal all the cavities. Tap the bottom of the molds on the work surface. Using the wall scraper, scrape the surplus chocolate off the top of the mold back into the bowl of chocolate. Refrigerate the molds until set, about 5 to 10 minutes. Refrigerate the leftover chocolate on waxed paper until set and store in an airtight container at room temperature for future use. Place a sheet of waxed paper on the work surface.

8. To release the chocolate from the mold: Tap the bottom of the mold once on the work surface. Turn it over onto the waxed paper, and the pieces should drop out easily. If they don't, flex the mold. Repeat to release the chocolate in the other molds.

Makes about 48 shells

A Chocolate Bowl

A chocolate bowl filled with just about anything *leaves an indelible impression on guests at the end of a beautiful evening. When I give a chocolate bowl as a gift, I often accompany it with a mallet tied with streamers, to show that the bowl is to be broken and eaten when empty. When selecting a mold, look for plastic or metal bowls with sloped sides and shiny, scratch-free interiors. (I have an inexpensive set that I use exclusively for this purpose.) Like other hollow-molding procedures, this one works best if you use couverture chocolate, which swirls easily, leaving a smooth surface on the interior of the bowl.*

> 1 ½ pounds semisweet couverture chocolate, coarsely chopped, plus 6 ounces semisweet couverture chocolate, in chunks (for tempering)

⁂ Swirling the chocolate in the mold.

1. Clear a 3-foot-wide area of work space. Have at hand a dampened reusable cleaning cloth, 2 sheets of waxed paper, and one 9¾-inch (8-cup) metal or plastic bowl to use as a mold.

2. Melt and temper the chopped chocolate (see page 22). Pour about ⅓ of it in the bottom of the mold, twisting and turning it to direct the swirl of chocolate to cover the entire surface, except for the rim. Add more chocolate, if necessary. Hold the coated mold in a partially inverted position over the bowl of tempered chocolate, vigorously shaking it from side to side to coax the excess chocolate to drain back into it. Turn the coated mold upright and slap the outside wall to smooth the surface and level the small amount of chocolate in the bottom. Wrap the tip of your index finger in a corner of the damp cloth and wipe the excess chocolate off the rim of the coated mold. Refrigerate until the chocolate is barely set, about 5 minutes. Don't refrigerate it longer, or the chocolate may crack. When not in use, place the bowl of excess chocolate in a pan or slightly larger bowl of warm (90°F) water, replenishing the warm water as needed. Stir the chocolate occasionally as you work, scraping the sides of the bowl. Dry the bottom of the bowl each time you remove it from the water.

continued

❧ Coating the entire mold surface, except the rim.

❧ Draining the excess chocolate.

a chocolate bowl, continued

3. To add a second layer, pour most of the excess chocolate in the bottom of the mold, swirling it over the surface again. Drain the excess chocolate back into the bowl, slap the outside of the mold, and wipe the rim. Refrigerate until the chocolate is completely set and the bottom of the mold feels cold, about 20 minutes.

4. Refrigerate the leftover chocolate on a sheet of waxed paper until set and store in an airtight container at room temperature for future use.

5. To release the chocolate, grasp the sides of the mold with both hands, with your thumbs bracing the bottom and your fingers curled over the edge. Invert the mold over the waxed paper–lined work surface, pressing the bottom gently with both thumbs, if necessary, to release the chocolate onto the paper. If it doesn't release, refrigerate the mold briefly and try again. If it doesn't release after an hour, the chocolate was improperly tempered and you will have to begin again (see page 22).

Makes one 9¾-inch bowl

❧ Wiping the excess chocolate off the rim of the mold.

❧ Releasing the set chocolate.

A Chocolate Box

Once you have gained some molding experience, you will be ready to mold hollow chocolate boxes and baskets in cake pans. Cake pans make excellent molds because they have deep cavities and come in a variety of shapes and sizes. If you use a straight-sided pan, you'll be able to mold a lid in it, too, because the diameter of the bottom of the pan is the same as the top.

1 ½ pounds white couverture chocolate, coarsely chopped, plus 6 ounces white couverture chocolate, in chunks (for tempering)

1. Clear a 3-foot-wide area of work space. Have at hand a small angled metal spatula, a dampened reusable cleaning cloth, a sheet of waxed paper, and two 6-by-2-inch straight-sided round cake pans.

2. Melt and temper the chopped chocolate (see page 22). When not in use, place the bowl of chocolate in a pan or a slightly larger bowl of warm (88°F) water, replenishing the warm water as needed. Stir the chocolate occasionally as you work, scraping the sides of the bowl. Dry the bottom of the bowl each time you remove it from the water.

3. Pour about 1 cup of chocolate in the bottom of a cake pan, twisting and turning it as you swirl the chocolate over the entire surface, except for the rim. Add more chocolate if necessary. Hold the coated pan in a partially inverted position over the bowl of melted chocolate to allow most of the excess chocolate to drain back into it and the rest to settle in the base. Turn the pan upright, slapping the outside wall to level the chocolate in the base. Wrap the tip of your index finger in the corner of the damp cloth and use it to wipe the chocolate off the rim. Refrigerate until the chocolate is barely dry, about 5 minutes. Don't refrigerate it longer, or the chocolate may crack.

Meanwhile, stir the melted chocolate, scraping the sides of the bowl.

4. Cradle the coated pan in the palm of your hand, close to and tilted toward the bowl of chocolate. Dip the bottom 2 inches of the spatula blade into the chocolate and apply it to the inside of the walls, as if frosting a cake, coating a 2-inch section. Using the edge of the blade, scrape the excess chocolate off the rim after each application. Turn the pan, keeping it at the same tilted angle. Continue to spread and scrape the chocolate until the inside walls are completely coated. Wipe the chocolate off the rim and refrigerate until the chocolate is barely dry, about 3 minutes.

5. Coat the inside walls of the pan again, scraping the rim after each application. Wipe the rim and refrigerate until the chocolate is completely set and the bottom feels cold, about 20 minutes.

6. To mold a lid, pour a rounded ½ cup of chocolate (about 6 ounces) in the bottom of the second pan. Tap the bottom of the pan on the work surface and refrigerate until the chocolate sets completely, about 15 to 20 minutes. To release the chocolate lid, grasp the pan with both hands, with your fingers touching the chocolate and your thumbs pressed against the bottom of the pan. Invert the pan over a sheet of waxed paper, pressing the bottom gently to release the chocolate.

7. To release the chocolate box, place both thumbs inside the pan, touching the chocolate-coated sides, with your fingers on the exterior. Pull the chocolate box straight up and out of the pan.

8. Refrigerate the leftover chocolate on a sheet of waxed paper until set and store in an airtight container at room temperature for future use.

Makes one 6-inch-diameter round box and one lid

Chocolate Cups

USING BALLOON MOLDS

You will get a bang out of using a balloon as a mold for chocolate—one way or another. On rare occasions, the bang may be literal, but if you're lucky, your kitchen will *not* be freshly painted, as mine was the day a balloon exploded in my face and on my walls. That experience didn't deter me from continuing to use balloons as molds, because, frankly, I think the odd explosion is a small price to pay for the enjoyment that this process gives me on other occasions. Here are some helpful tips for making your experiences pleasant:

Select inexpensive balloons with shiny surfaces that are not coated in talc. Wipe them with a damp cloth and air-dry before using.

Experiment with different brands of balloons, since some release better than others. If the balloon sticks to the chocolate, jiggle it gently. If it doesn't release, discard the whole thing.

Dip balloons in tempered chocolate or *cool* confectionery coating to minimize the chance of an explosion. Inflating them 30 minutes before you dip them also seems to help.

Dip balloons in fluid melted chocolate or coating, rather than in thick, heavy melted chocolate.

Deflate and remove the balloon as soon as the chocolate sets. Some balloons can be used twice.

These simple little cups, which can be used in many ways, are the foundation for the charming birdbath dessert on page 124. Using a balloon to mold cups and saucers will enable you to vary their size and depth simply by inflating or deflating the balloon or by plunging the balloon to various depths in the chocolate. The balloons are easier to deflate if you secure them with 1-inch-wide metal bulldog clips, which are ordinarily used to grip and hang papers on a hook. They are available at office supply stores. These chocolate cups store well for months, stacked between waxed paper in an airtight container, at a moderate room temperature.

> 2 pounds semisweet chocolate, coarsely chopped, plus 8 ounces semisweet chocolate, in chunks (for tempering)

1. Clear a 3-foot-wide area of work surface and line it with waxed paper. Have ready eight 5-inch round balloons and one 9¾-inch (8-cup) shallow mixing bowl. Inflate 8 balloons to measure approximately 3¾ inches in diameter. Secure the open ends with the bulldog clips, or twist and knot them. Wipe the balloons with a damp cloth and air-dry them. Line 2 large rimless baking sheets with waxed paper, securing it with tape. Clear space in the refrigerator to accommodate the baking sheets and the 6-inch-high inflated balloons.

2. Melt and temper the chopped chocolate (see page 22) in the shallow bowl. Place the bowl on a folded towel to buffer the coolness of the work surface. Stir the chocolate occasionally, scraping the sides of the bowl.

❧ Plunging the balloon into the chocolate.

❧ Jiggling the balloon to drain excess chocolate.

3. Holding a balloon by the top end, gently plunge the rounded base about 1⅛ inches deep straight down into the chocolate. Immediately lift the balloon and jiggle it gently over the bowl of chocolate to coax the excess chocolate to drain back into it. Set the base of the wet balloon on a waxed paper–lined baking sheet, allowing room for 3 more dipped balloons spaced 2 inches apart. Without delay, dip the remaining balloons until the chocolate is too shallow for dipping, filling both baking sheets. Refrigerate until the chocolate sets and feels cold, about 10 minutes.

4. To release a balloon, pinch the open end closed while releasing the clip to allow the balloon to pull away slowly from the chocolate cup. If knotted, pinch the open end closed while snipping a tiny hole near the top with sharp-pointed scissors. If a cup has a hole in the bottom, place it back on the lined baking sheet and plug it with a small dollop of leftover chocolate. (It won't show once the cup is filled.)

5. Pour the leftover chocolate onto a sheet of waxed paper, refrigerate until set, and store in an airtight container at room temperature for future use.

Makes 8 cups

VARIATIONS:

Banana Boat Cups (for banana splits): Hold a 6-inch-long balloon by both ends and dip it halfway into the bowl of chocolate. Lift it, shake it gently over the bowl, and place it on a lined baking sheet. Proceed as directed in the main recipe.

Flower Petal Cups (for mousse, fruit, or ice cream): Stand a round balloon in the center of the surface of a bowl of chocolate and rock it forward and back to an upright position to form the first petal. Rotate the balloon one-quarter turn and repeat to make 4 more petals. Place on a waxed paper–lined baking sheet. Proceed as directed in the main recipe.

To make marbleized flower petal cups, follow the marbleizing instructions on page 39, using 2 pounds white couverture chocolate for the pool of chocolate and 1 pound semisweet chocolate for the stripes.

Chocolate Note

Two pounds of chocolate may seem like a lot to make 8 cups weighing 1 ounce each, but you need that much volume to plunge the balloons to a depth of 1⅛ inches. (Two pounds of solid chocolate equals only 3 cups of melted chocolate.)

Chocolate Leaves

Thick, shiny leaves with distinct vein markings on their underside make the prettiest chocolate mirror images. My favorites are lemon leaves, a misnomer for salal leaves, available by the stem in most flower shops. Each stem contains several leaves in a variety of sizes. The leaves are sturdy enough to use more than once and will keep, refrigerated, for several weeks.

Like other nontoxic leaves, lemon (salal) leaves may be used in combination with chocolate provided you soak, scrub, rinse, and dry them thoroughly before using. Other acceptable choices include gardenia, grape ivy (not English ivy), magnolia, rose, and real lemon leaves.

Toxic leaves that you should avoid using are amaryllis (jonquil, daffodil, narcissus), caladium, delphinium (larkspur), dieffenbachia, English ivy, holly, hydrangea, lily of the valley, mistletoe, oleander, poinsettia, poppy, and rhododendron (laurel, azalea). Consult a botanical book or a local horticultural expert to guide your other choices.

> 8 ounces semisweet chocolate, coarsely chopped, plus one 2-ounce chunk semisweet chocolate (for tempering)

1. Select 12 nontoxic fresh leaves, each about 2 inches wide by 3 inches long. At least 1 hour ahead, soak the leaves in warm water. Scrub both sides with a vegetable brush, rinse thoroughly, and air-dry on paper towels.

2. Clear a 3-foot-wide area of work surface, lining it with waxed paper. Spread the leaves out on the paper, face down. Line a large rimless baking sheet with waxed paper, taping it in place. Have at hand a small, angled metal spatula and a small pair of sharp, pointed scissors.

3. Melt and temper the chocolate (see page 22). Place the bowl in a pan or a slightly larger bowl of warm (90°F) water, replenishing it with more warm water as needed. Stir the chocolate occasionally as you work, scraping the sides of the bowl.

4. Hold a leaf face down, resting on your open hand and supported on top with your thumb. Using the small metal spatula, scoop and spread a dollop of chocolate across the underside of the leaf, covering it completely. Examine the thick part of the vein nearest the stem to see if it is thickly coated. If not, dab it with more chocolate. Clean the edges of the leaf with your fingertips. Place it chocolate-side-up on the waxed paper–lined baking sheet. Repeat with the remaining leaves. Refrigerate until the chocolate sets completely, about 5 to 10 minutes.

5. Beginning at the stem, gently pull the fresh leaf away from the chocolate leaf. If the point breaks, wait until the chocolate leaf returns to room temperature, then reshape it with the scissors.

6. Use the leftover chocolate to make more leaves, or pour it onto a sheet of waxed paper, refrigerate until set, and store in an airtight container at room temperature for future use.

Makes 12 to 24 leaves

Chocolate Note
You can alter the shape and size of a plain leaf by cutting it with a pair of small, pointed scissors. To do so, fold the leaf in half along the center vein, so that whatever shape you cut will be mirrored by the other half (see page 118).

RED MAPLE

SUGAR MAPLE

POPLAR

GARDENIA

BLACK OAK

ROSE

WHITE OAK

USING FREEZER PAPER AND ACETATE AS MOLDS

Rolls of polycoated freezer paper are among the most versatile "molds." The paper is flexible enough to bend, yet heavy enough to hold its shape, even when coated with chocolate, and its glassine surface leaves a soft, lustrous gloss on the chocolate that is really quite beautiful. You can cut freezer paper into strips and then roll, bend, or twist it to create an endless variety of decorative shapes and forms: chocolate cylinders, cones, ribbons, bows, cake bands, corkscrews, and more. And there is no cleanup. Once the chocolate is set, you simply peel off the paper and throw it away.

Acetate, a clear plastic material, can be substituted for freezer paper when a higher chocolate shine is desired. Acetate (or Mylar) strips, which are traditionally used by bakers to protect the sides of boxed whipped cream cakes, are available through bakery suppliers and at many cake decorating stores. Sheets of it, which can be cut to suit your needs, are sold at office supply stores.

❧ Attaching the tapered ends of the loops to the pattern board.

❧ Attaching the second row of loops.

Chocolate Bows

It's easy to make chocolate bows that rival the ones on gift packages. You'll need extra work space for this project, which is necessarily a bit messy, but the results will make the cleanup worthwhile. When I was developing this technique, I found it helpful to have a real bow in front of me to guide me in assembly.

It takes 15 or 16 chocolate loops to make a bow, each one made on a strip of freezer paper. Each strip is coated with chocolate, left until partially set, and then pinched at the ends to form loops.

To assemble the bow, 11 or 12 loops are arranged in 2 concentric circles, joined together with piped dollops of chocolate. The open cavity in the center is plugged with a marshmallow to give the 3 or 4 loops that will be inserted there more height.

> 1 ½ pounds white chocolate, coarsely chopped, plus 6 ounces white chocolate, in chunks (for tempering)
>
> 1 large marshmallow, cut in half crosswise (see Note)

1. Fold one 10-inch-long sheet of polycoated freezer paper lengthwise into thirds, each measuring 10 by 5 inches. Slit the 2 creases with a knife, leaving the 3 sheets stacked. Using a ruler, mark off and cut ten 1-inch segments along the length of the strip, creating thirty 1-by-5-inch strips (which includes extras). Taper the ends of 20 strips to measure ¼ inch wide. Cut the remaining strips diagonally at one end to form the ends of the ribbons.

2. Clear a 3-by-2-foot area of work surface, covering it with sheets of waxed paper. Arrange 12 tapered strips on the paper, shiny-side-up, spaced several inches apart in 2 or 3 vertical rows. Line the backs of 2 large baking sheets and 1 pattern board with waxed paper. Have at hand a small, angled metal spatula and 4 or 5 parchment decorating bags.

3. Melt and temper the chopped chocolate (see page 22). Place the bowl in a pan or a slightly larger bowl of warm (88°F) water, replenishing it with more warm water as needed. Stir the chocolate occasionally, scraping the sides of the bowl.

4. Spoon some of the chocolate into a parchment bag, filling it half full (see page 11). Cut a ¼-inch opening in the tip of the bag. Squeezing hard, pipe a ½-inch-thick line of chocolate across the length of each strip. Using the angled spatula, spread the chocolate across the strips, beyond the edges and onto the waxed paper. Pull each strip away from the surface, leaving the surplus behind. Clean the edges with your fingertips and let the strip sit nearby until the chocolate is barely set but still malleable.

continued

chocolate bows, continued

5. To shape the loops, press the tapered ends together, coated surfaces touching. Stand them on their sides on the lined baking sheet. Refrigerate until set, about 10 minutes. Peel the paper off the chocolate.

6. Meanwhile, set the chocolate-coated sheets aside and line the work surface with more waxed paper. Stir the bowl of chocolate, scraping the sides of the bowl.

7. Fill another parchment bag, coating the remaining strips with chocolate. Loop the 8 tapered strips. Press the others against the paper-lined baking sheet in 2 or 3 places, chocolate-side down, forming ruffled strips. Refrigerate until set. Carefully peel the paper off the chocolate loops and strips.

8. To assemble the bow, fill a parchment bag with chocolate and cut a ¼-inch opening in the tip. Attach the tapered end of the first loop to the pattern board with a piped dollop of chocolate. Repeat with 5 more loops, forming a 5½-inch-diameter circle with a 1-inch-diameter opening in the center. Plug the opening with half of the marshmallow, attaching it to the paper with a dollop of chocolate, cut-side-down.

9. For the second row, center the tapered ends of 5 or 6 loops between those in the first row, attaching them with piped dollops of chocolate. Cover the marshmallow with more piped chocolate, filling in the center of the bow with 3 or 4 more loops, totaling 15 or 16 loops. Refrigerate the bow until set, about 5 to 10 minutes.

10. Clean the angled spatula and slide it under the bow to release it from the paper. Use the bow now, or store it in an airtight container at room temperature for up to 8 months.

11. Pour any leftover chocolate onto a sheet of waxed paper and refrigerate until set. Store in an airtight container at room temperature, along with the surplus chocolate from the waxed paper.

Chocolate Note
You may substitute a 1-ounce ball of white chocolate clay (page 77) or a whittled 1-inch-diameter chunk of white chocolate for the marshmallow.

piping chocolate

Knowing how to handle a decorating bag filled with chocolate is liberating! It enables you to fill molds, drizzle lines on dipped truffles, pipe designs, trace over patterns, flood areas, and do all kinds of fancy things with chocolate.

There is a noticeable difference between piping with tempered chocolate and piping with untempered chocolate or confectionery coating. Tempered chocolate has "body" (it is viscous), so the piped lines hold their shape, even when piped on the walls of a cake pan or inflated balloon. They will flatten, however, if you bump or touch them before they dry. Untempered melted chocolate and warm confectionery coating are fluid (not viscous), so piped lines flatten and letters run together easily, even when you don't bump them, and they dissolve into a puddle when you do. To minimize that problem, stir 3 or 4 ounces of solid pieces of confectionery coating into every pound of warm melted coating. Doing so tempers the coating, making it easier to use.

For piping with chocolate, there is no acceptable substitute for disposable decorating bags made of parchment paper (see page 9). Don't even *think* of substituting waxed paper, butcher paper, plastic food storage bags, or plastic squirt bottles for parchment paper unless you are willing to accept the frustrations that inevitably come with using them. For piping thick mixtures like truffle fillings, mousse, frosting, and whipped cream, I suggest using disposable clear plastic bags or reusable pastry bags (see page 14).

USING A PARCHMENT BAG

1. For most piping purposes, cut a $1/16$- to $1/4$-inch piece off the tip of the bag. The farther back from the tip you cut, the larger the hole and the thicker the piped line of chocolate (though the amount of pressure you put on the bag affects the thickness, too). If the opening is too small, cut off another tiny piece to make it larger. If it's too large, or if the chocolate begins to leak, place that bag inside another parchment bag, close it, cut the tip, and begin again. Use larger openings for filling molds and other utilitarian purposes, and smaller openings for piping delicate fine-line designs.

2. Cup the top of the bag in the palm of your hand as if it were a ball about to be thrown, with your thumb securing the rolled top in a locked position and your fingers gripping it in a horizontal position. Using your free hand, place your index finger 1 inch above the tip on the side of the bag to guide, steady, and support your working hand as you pipe. Keep your elbows close to your body or braced against the edge of the work surface.

3. To unplug a chocolate-filled decorating bag, pinch the opening between your fingertips to force out the obstacle, usually a hard particle of dry chocolate. If a larger plug has formed, hold the tip of the bag against the side of a warm pan to soften the chocolate, then pinch the tip and/or squeeze the bag to force it out. Alternatively, warm the tip with a hair dryer.

Let the chocolate set inside the parchment bags, then discard the bags and store the leftover chocolate in an airtight container at room temperature for future use.

Piping Lines of Chocolate

1. Rotate your wrist to the right slightly (or to the left, if you're left-handed) to allow a clearer field of vision as you pipe. Hold the bag at a 30-degree angle to the piping surface, with the tip barely touching it. Squeeze the bag gently to start the flow of chocolate. The harder you squeeze the bag, the faster the flow and the faster you must move the bag. If you remain in one position while squeezing the bag, a mound of chocolate will form.

2. To halt the flow of chocolate, stop squeezing the bag, make a brief contact with the surface, and rotate the tip clockwise, positioning the opening so that it is parallel with the previously piped line in case a stray drop of chocolate should fall as you pull the tip away.

Piping Beads and Bulbs of Chocolate

Tempered chocolate has the ability to swell and hold its shape when you pipe with it, which enables you to pipe swans, grape clusters, beads, bulbs, and many other dimensional shapes. I use chocolate beads and bulbs (large beads) to form borders for many of my boxes, bowls, plaques, and serving platters.

1. Using a spoon or rubber spatula, fill a parchment bag half full with chocolate. Cut a ⅛-inch opening in the tip. Use a larger opening for piping bulbs.

2. Hold the bag at a 45-degree angle to the piping surface with the tip barely touching it. Squeeze the bag, allowing the force of the emerging chocolate to lift the tip off the surface. Maintain a steady pressure on the bag, holding that position long enough for the bead of chocolate to swell and fan out. Relax the pressure on the bag as you lower the tip to the surface, pulling it away sharply enough to cause the end of the piped bead to taper to a point. Begin each new bead on the tip of the "tail" of the previous one, forming a border of beads or bulbs.

Piping Chocolate over a Pattern

Most of us need a little help when it comes to piping designs free-hand on chocolate. Using a pattern enables us to trace over a design with chocolate and then transfer it to the surface of a cake or molded piece of chocolate after it sets.

There are thousands of patterns to be found in coloring, embroidery, arts and crafts, and cake decorating books. You can also make your own patterns with the help of a template, a small T-square, a ruler, and quad-ruled paper, which are all sold in office supply stores. A copy machine can enlarge or reduce the size of the patterns to suit your needs.

I use waxed paper–covered pattern boards (see page 15) for many purposes, but of course they are best suited for this work. Patterns drawn on standard 8½-by-11-inch paper will slip under the paper-lined boards perfectly, making it easy for you to trace over the designs with chocolate. If you don't have any, substitute a rimless or inverted sided baking sheet lined with waxed paper, securing 2 sides of the paper with tape (to enable you to slip the pattern under it).

Once the chocolate-piped design is set, you must release it from the paper promptly, or it will contract and curl up along the edges. To prevent that, slide a small, angled spatula along the edges of the piped design to loosen it from the paper as soon as the chocolate in that area appears to be dry.

Etching a Pattern on Chocolate

Patterns can also be used to etch a design or words directly onto the surface of a molded piece of chocolate with a sharp, pointed object like an ice pick, a nail, a darning needle, or a scriber tool (see page 15). This technique, which is described on page 99, will enable you to pipe chocolate over the etched pattern with the skill and confidence of an experienced master confectioner.

modeling chocolate clay

Corn syrup can transform a bowl of melted chocolate into a claylike material so malleable that it can be rolled, cut, shaped, woven, and modeled very much like the real thing, but with one important difference: You can eat it! Here are some tips for making perfect chocolate clay:

Do not use chocolate chips or expensive imported chocolate for making clay.

Weigh the chocolate on a scale. Melt it carefully so that it does not exceed 100°F. (It is not necessary to temper it.)

Use a liquid measuring cup, such as a Pyrex glass cup with a spout, to measure the corn syrup; rinse the cup first with cold water.

View the cup measurement line at eye level.

To get an accurate measurement, scrape all the corn syrup into the chocolate with a rubber spatula.

Stir and fold the two mixtures together in a shallow medium bowl to give yourself room to lift and manipulate the mass so that no area is neglected.

Dark Chocolate Clay

Chocolate clay is used for many purposes, so I always try to have some around for unexpected needs—which is why I often double the recipe when I make it. A freshly made batch of dark chocolate clay is ready to use when it feels firm and breaks apart when you bend it. Once you knead it, it will become malleable enough to model flower petals and weave baskets, but it will firm up again when it cools to room temperature. Unfortunately, heat and humidity are not conducive to working with chocolate clay. If you live in that kind of climate, you must always work with clay in an air-conditioned room. Nevertheless, the finished clay pieces will always remain soft and a little sticky.

10 ounces semisweet chocolate,
   coarsely chopped

⅓ cup light corn syrup

1. In a shallow medium bowl, melt the chocolate (see page 16) without heating it above 100°F. Add the corn syrup. Using a rubber spatula, stir and fold the mixture, scraping the sides and bottom of the bowl well, until no shiny syrup is visible and the mixture forms a thick ball. Do not overmix it.

2. Turn the clay out onto a sheet of waxed paper. Using the rubber spatula, pat it into a 7-inch square. Let it sit uncovered at room temperature until firm, about 2 hours. Use the clay at once, or store in an airtight container at room temperature for up to 1 month.

Makes about 13 ounces clay

VARIATIONS:

Milk Chocolate, White Chocolate, or Confectionery Coating Clay: Use 10 ounces chocolate or coating and a *scant* ⅓ cup light corn syrup. Let sit several hours until firm.

Chocolate Note
Since all chocolates vary so much, you may have to adjust the quantities used in this recipe the second time you make it. To make a firmer, less sticky clay, use a little more chocolate (or slightly less corn syrup). To make a softer clay, use slightly less chocolate (or a little more corn syrup).

Chocolate Clay Roses

Chocolate roses are worth the little effort they require, when you consider their decorative value on chocolate cakes, edible boxes, and baskets. There is no need to panic at the thought of creating a rose from a lump of chocolate clay. The lesson is purely academic. If you can follow instructions, you can make a rose.

It takes 9 petals to make a rose, each made from a ball of clay. The size of the ball will determine the size of the petal and the size of the rose. To make a 2-inch rose, the balls should be the size of hazelnuts.

When flattened, the balls should be round, about 1 inch in diameter, and paper thin along the top edge, thickening gradually to ¼ inch at the bottom.

Each rose consists of a cone-shaped tepee and 2 rows of petals. There are 3 petals in the first row and 5 in the second. To make a 3-inch rose, you will need a third row of 7 additional petals.

continued

❧ Pressing the clay balls.

❧ Lifting the petal.

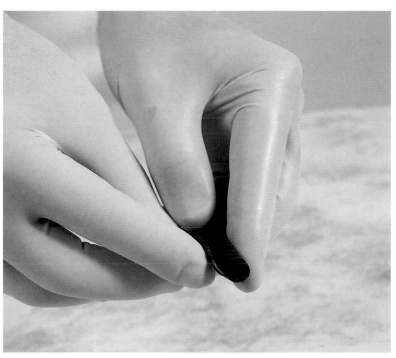

❧ Forming the tepee shape.

❧ Wrapping the second petal around the tepee.

chocolate clay roses, continued

Dark Chocolate Clay (page 77)

1. Clear a 3-foot-wide smooth work surface. Have at hand two 1-gallon-size plastic storage bags (not the heavy-duty reclosable kind).

2. Using the heel of your hand, knead a handful of dry, firm chocolate clay on the work surface until it is the consistency of Play-Doh: soft and malleable, but not sticky.

3. Lay one of the plastic storage bags flat on the work surface. Break off and roll small pieces of clay into ½-inch-diameter balls (about the size of hazelnuts). Arrange them in rows, spaced 1 inch apart, covering the entire surface of the bag. Lay the other bag on top of the balls, covering them completely.

4. To make the 9 petals for each rose, place the tip of your index finger on the top half of one of the balls, aiming it directly at the surface of the bag. Press it 3 times—first in the center and then on either side—flattening the ball into a 1-inch round petal. Press the top edge 2 or 3 more times to make it paper thin, leaving the bottom of the petal about ¼ inch thick. Repeat with each of the remaining balls. Remove the top bag.

5. Lift the first petal by its thick bottom edge, holding it between your thumb and index finger so that the thin edge of the petal is facing up. To form the tepee shape, which is the center of the rose, place the tip of your other index finger under the top edge of the petal, pointing toward the center. Nudge that portion of the petal forward, coaxing it to roll over onto itself, forming the first half of the tepee. Using your other fingertip, roll the opposite edge of the petal the same way, pushing it forward so that it meets and slightly overlaps the other half to form a tepee with a small hole at the top and a larger, thicker one at the bottom. Don't fuss with its appearance; very little of it will show in the completed rose.

6. Center the second petal over the door of the tepee, positioning it so that the top edge is even with the top of the tepee. Gently wrap the sides of the second petal around the tepee without distorting its cone shape. Using the tip of your index finger, roll the right edge of the petal downward, curling it slightly. Turn the bud counterclockwise and attach the third petal, overlapping the second one and positioning it so their top edges are even. Curl the right edge of the third petal. Turn the bud counterclockwise again. Attach and curl a fourth petal the same way.

7. For the second row, center a fifth petal over 2 petals in the first row, positioning it so that its top edge is even with the rest. Curl both sides of the petal this time, causing it to open slightly. Continue overlapping, attaching, and curling the sides of the last 4 petals to complete the full rose. Pinch off any excess clay at the base of the rose and use it to make more balls.

8. Repeat to make more roses until the clay is used up. Use the roses at once, or air-dry them on a waxed paper–lined surface for several days before storing in an airtight container at room temperature for up to 1 year.

Makes about 12 roses

Chocolate Notes
If the clay balls or petals become too soft from your body heat to handle, let sit at room temperature for at least 10 minutes. To cool your hands, periodically grasp a cold glass or immerse your hands in ice water. Dry your hands well before touching the clay again.

To make a rosebud, attach 3 petals to a tepee. To make a half rose, attach 4 petals to a tepee.

❧ Finished roses.

Chocolate Clay Gardenias

Making clay gardenias or roses involves a series of repetitious steps that culminate in the creation of one glorious flower. Set aside some uninterrupted time to practice making a few gardenias to see what I mean. It may strike you as being laborious to make a multipetaled flower now, but when you see how easy it is to make one, you'll quickly change your opinion. Besides, 1 gardenia and a couple of buds are usually sufficient to decorate the top of an entire cake or chocolate box.

It takes 16 petals for a gardenia, each made from a ball of confectionery clay. The size of the ball will determine the size of the petal and the size of the gardenia. To make a 3½-inch-diameter gardenia, the balls should be the size of marbles, about ⅝ of an inch.

When flattened, the balls should be round, about 1 ¼ inches in diameter, paper thin along the top edge and thickening gradually to ¼ inch at the bottom.

Each gardenia consists of 2 rows of petals arranged in concentric circles, with a 5-petal bud inserted in the center as a final step. The petals are joined together with piped dollops of melted confectionery coating.

White Confectionery Coating Clay
(page 77)

4 ounces white confectionery coating

1. Clear a 3-foot-wide smooth work surface. Have at hand two 1-gallon-size plastic storage bags (not the heavy-duty reclosable kind). Line a pattern board with waxed paper (see page 15).

2. Using the heel of your hand, knead a handful of clay on the work surface until it is the consistency of Play-Doh: soft and malleable, but not sticky. Lay one of the plastic bags flat on the work surface. Break off and roll 16 small pieces of clay into marble-sized balls, about ⅝ inch in diameter. Arrange them in rows, spaced 2 inches apart, covering the entire surface of the bag. Lay the other bag on top of the balls, covering them completely.

3. Place the tip of your index finger on the top half of a ball, aiming it directly at the surface of the bag. Press it 3 times— first in the center and then on either side—flattening the ball into a 1¼-inch round petal. Press the top edge 2 or 3 more times to make it paper thin, leaving the bottom of the petal about ¼ inch thick. Repeat with each of the remaining balls. Remove the top bag.

4. Lift the first 2 petals by their thick bottom edges, holding one in each hand with the thin edges up. Bend the petals in half lengthwise to resemble Mexican tacos in an upright position. Holding the open ends facing inward, interlock the petals to form the bud. Using the tip of your thumb, roll back the outer edge of each petal. Set aside.

5. To shape the remaining 14 petals, hold the thick bottom part of a petal between the index fingers and thumbs of both hands. Taper it to a point by pinching it between the tips of both index fingers, causing the petal to cup slightly. Gently roll the thin top edges of the petal downward along both sides. Repeat to shape the remaining petals. Surround the bud with 3 evenly spaced petals, pressing gently to make them adhere.

6. Melt the coating (see page 18). Spoon it into a parchment bag, cutting a ¼-inch opening in the tip. Pipe the coating in a thick 1¾-inch-diameter circle on the pattern board. For the first row, press the tapered ends of 6 petals into the wet coating, spaced evenly apart. Pipe a little coating on top to secure them. For the second row, place the tapered ends of 5 or 6 more petals in the wet coating between the petals in the first row, keeping the center cavity open. Fill the center with coating.

7. Insert a toothpick into the throat of the 5-petal bud to enable you to lift it, turn it upside down, and hold it there while pinching, cutting, and removing the excess clay from the bottom. With the toothpick's help, place the bud in the center of the flower. Discard the toothpick and refrigerate the flower until the coating sets, about 5 to 10 minutes.

8. Repeat to make 5 more gardenias. If the coating-filled parchment bag needs rewarming, place it in the microwave on low (30 percent) power for about 10 seconds, to just soften it.

9. Use the gardenias at once, or air-dry them on a waxed paper–lined surface for several days, then store in an airtight container at room temperature for up to 1 year.

Makes 6 gardenias

VARIATIONS:

Chocolate Clay Leaves: Tint a portion of the clay green with a few dots of food coloring (see page 13) applied with a toothpick. Using a rolling pin, flatten the clay into a thin sheet on a waxed paper–covered pattern board (see page 15). Using a small leaf cutter or craft knife, cut out 5 leaves, each 1½ inches long. Press the surface with a clean toothpick to mark the veins. Tuck the leaves around the base of the gardenia.

Gardenia Buds in Two Sizes: Make 9 more petals. Proceed as directed to shape them into 2 "tacos." Surround one "taco" with 3 petals and the other with 2. Trim the excess clay from the bottoms.

marble slab/countertop work

Marble is an excellent surface for cooling chocolate and candy syrups (see page 55) and for making beautiful decorations. If you don't have one, substitute a piece of granite, a plastic-laminated countertop such as Corian or Formica, or the back of a heavy metal baking sheet. Unfortunately, except for granite, none of those surfaces has the quick cooling effect of marble, so waiting for chocolate to dry on them can really test your patience. If you are serious about working with chocolate, I urge you to invest in a piece of marble or granite that is at least 18 by 24 inches (see page 14).

Here are a few tips on working on marble:

The temperature of the room affects the temperature of the work surface. Ideally, the room should be 68° to 70°F. A cooler room will cause the chocolate to set before you can do anything with it. If the room is too warm, the chocolate will take forever to set.

To make tree bark, bands, ruffles, twigs, and other decorations on a marble surface, you must use tempered melted chocolate.

To make decorations with confectionery coating, a plastic-laminated work surface is actually preferred.

To work with marble, you'll need an angled metal spatula and 3- and 6-inch-wide wall scrapers with flexible blades to spread and scrape the chocolate on and off the surface. The width of the blade ultimately determines the maximum width of the chocolate pieces.

To make striped pieces of chocolate, you'll need a square-notched adhesive spreader (my preference) or a standard cake-decorating comb.

Until you gain experience, always work on a small area of the marble at a time; otherwise, some sections may set up before you are able to get to them. The cooler the room, the faster the chocolate will set, and the faster you must work.

It takes patience to work with chocolate on a marble surface because of variables that are beyond your control. Choose a quiet day for experimenting.

Chocolate Tree Bark

A talented young woman from Argentina shared this technique with me when she was a student in my class at the Wilton School of Confectionery Art. Years later, I encountered similar pieces of chocolate tree bark in Spain, where they are called leña *(kindling wood), and packaged for gifts in miniature wheelbarrows. I use multiple pieces of chocolate tree bark to create realistic driftwood centerpieces, cake decorations, and unusual chocolate baskets to fill with cookies and candy. You'll find it very hard to resist nibbling a few pieces as you make them, for at that moment the chocolate is just barely dry but still soft enough to melt in your mouth.*

1 pound milk chocolate, coarsely chopped, plus 4 ounces milk chocolate, in chunks (for tempering)

1. Clear a 3-foot-wide area of work surface. If you have a marble slab, place it in front of you, with the longest side parallel with the edge of the work surface. Otherwise, select an alternative work surface (see page 14), cleaning and drying it thoroughly. Have at hand an angled metal spatula, a baking sheet, and 3- and 6-inch wall scrapers.

2. Melt and temper the chopped chocolate (see page 22). When not in use, keep the bowl in a pan or a slightly larger bowl of warm (88°F) water, replenishing the warm water as needed. Stir the chocolate occasionally, scraping the sides of the bowl. Dry the bottom of the bowl each time you remove it from the water.

3. Pour about ½ cup of chocolate in the center of the work surface. Spread it horizontally with the angled spatula and then vertically with the 6-inch wall scraper until it is slightly less than 1⁄16 inch thick.

4. Let set until the chocolate no longer looks wet, about 3 minutes in a 72°F room. Touch it lightly with your fingertip. It is ready when the chocolate feels barely dry and your finger no longer smudges the surface.

5. Immediately grasp the handle of the 3-inch wall scraper, palm down. Position the scraper at a 20-degree angle to the surface, beginning in the lower right-hand corner. (Use the opposite side if you're left-handed.) Place your other thumb across the width of the blade, about 1 inch from the bottom. Push the blade forward about 6 inches. The chocolate will bunch together against your thumb, forming a pleated log resembling tree bark. If the pleats appear wet and indistinguishable, the chocolate is not sufficiently dry. Wait 1 minute, or try a different area along the perimeter. For a thicker piece, push the blade forward from end to end. For a thinner piece, push it forward a shorter distance. For wider pieces, use the 6-inch wall scraper.

6. Slide the blade under the chocolate log to lift and place it on the baking sheet. Repeat to make more bark, working quickly before the chocolate gets too dry and the pleats begin to splinter. If they do, scrape the chocolate off the marble, set the shreds aside to remelt later, pour another pool of chocolate, and begin again. With practice, you should be able to make about 10 small pieces of tree bark from each pool of chocolate.

7. Use the pieces at once, or store at room temperature in an airtight container for up to 10 months. Store the leftover scraps of chocolate in an airtight container at room temperature for future use.

continued

chocolate tree bark, continued

❧ Spreading the chocolate horizontally with the angled spatula.

❧ Spreading the chocolate vertically with the wall scraper.

❧ Creating pleats in the chocolate.

Chocolate Cutouts

You can make simple decorations for cakes, desserts, and edible containers by spreading chocolate in a thin sheet on a perfectly flat waxed paper–lined baking sheet, letting it set, and then cutting it with a sharp craft-type knife or cookie cutters.

> 4 ounces white chocolate, coarsely chopped, plus one 1-ounce chunk white chocolate (for tempering)

1. Clear a 3-foot-wide smooth work surface. Line a large, flat, rimless baking sheet with waxed paper, securing it with tape. Have at hand a single sheet of plastic cut from a 1-gallon-size plastic storage bag, an angled metal spatula, a ruler or template and craft-type knife with a thin blade, or a small cookie cutter (see Note).

2. Melt and temper the chopped chocolate (see page 22).

3. Pour the chocolate into the center of the baking sheet. Using the angled metal spatula, spread it in a $^1/_{16}$-inch-thick layer. Tap the bottom of the baking sheet on the work surface sharply to smooth the top and level the surface of the chocolate. Refrigerate until the chocolate is just barely set, about 5 minutes. Once the chocolate begins to set, you must work quickly. If the chocolate gets too cold and/or dry, it will become brittle and splinter when you cut it. Immediately slide the metal spatula under the edges of the chocolate to prevent the sides from curling up.

4. Let sit until the chocolate warms to room temperature, about 15 minutes. To cut strips of chocolate, use a ruler or template and a craft knife. To cut shapes with cookie cutters, cover the chocolate with the plastic sheet. Place the cutter on top of the plastic. Press firmly to cut the chocolate surface through the plastic, usually without tearing it. The chocolate pieces will have rounded edges.

5. Store the leftover pieces of chocolate in an airtight container at room temperature for future use.

Chocolate Note
Small gum paste cutters are perfect for cutting out chocolate designs (see page 13).

tinting white chocolate and confectionary coating

As beautiful as white chocolate is, you can enhance it and confectionery coating by adding small amounts of oil-based food coloring gel, powder, or liquid candy colors (see page 13). If you use a water- or alcohol-based food coloring, it is apt to thicken the chocolate or coating.

1. Place up to 1 cup of tempered melted white chocolate or melted white confectionery coating in a small bowl. Use a small metal spatula to add a little food coloring to the chocolate or coating along the perimeter of the bowl.

2. Using the spatula, work the food coloring into a small portion of the chocolate or coating, stroking it against the wall of the bowl. Gradually blend the tinted portion into the remaining chocolate or coating with a rubber spatula. To deepen the color, repeat the procedure.

Chocolate Note
To produce incredibly beautiful muted shades that are perfect for fall and winter decorations (see page 92), mix red or green food coloring with milk chocolate clay.

Chocolate Spaghetti Twigs and Branches

One day, while I was looking for new ways to use chocolate, I stumbled on the idea of infusing spaghetti with unsweetened cocoa powder. Since then, I have had a great time experimenting with different types of pastas in all kinds of decorative ways. When the strands harden, they bear a striking resemblance to real twigs and branches.

4 ½ cups water

½ cup unsweetened cocoa powder

2 ounces spaghetti

1. Line 2 large baking sheets with aluminum foil and coat them lightly with vegetable-oil cooking spray.

2. In a small saucepan, whisk 1½ cups of the water together with the cocoa until well blended. Cook over medium heat until the cocoa dissolves. Remove from heat and pour into a 10-inch pie plate.

3. In a medium saucepan, boil the remaining 3 cups water. Add the spaghetti and bring to a second boil. Cook for 3 or 4 minutes, just to soften the strands. Drain the spaghetti in a colander.

4. Lay the spaghetti in the cocoa water, shifting the strands around to assure that they are all submerged. Let steep in the water, stirring occasionally, until the strands turn a medium-dark brown, about 1 hour.

5. Preheat the oven to 200°F. Drain the spaghetti in a colander. Divide the strands between the 2 baking sheets, arranging them so they do not touch. Dry the strands in the oven for 1 hour. Remove from the oven and release them from the foil. Put them back in the oven, piled in a heap, turn off the oven, and let the spaghetti dry for about 20 minutes.

6. Let cool, then store in an airtight container at room temperature for up to 1 year. If the strands appear dull, spray them lightly with vegetable-oil cooking spray just before using.

Makes 4 ounces chocolate spaghetti

VARIATION:

Green Spaghetti Twigs: Substitute 1 teaspoon green liquid food coloring for the cocoa. Proceed as directed in the main recipe.

5

spectacular chocolate gifts

boxes, bowls, baskets, and centerpieces

Serving something made of chocolate in its own chocolate container is the quintessential form of packaging for those who are seriously chocolate-inclined! I love to see the reaction that some of my chocolate gifts inspire when the recipient realizes that the container is as edible as what's inside. The reactions range from disbelief to downright uncontrollable gluttony.

Now that you're a little more experienced, you can make some of those same gifts yourself, using techniques discussed earlier in the book along with a few new ones. Don't let the complicated appearance of the finished pieces intimidate you. Each one is made up of several steps, none of which is difficult. All of the boxes, bowls, baskets, and centerpieces in this chapter can be made in stages, months before you need them. Once made, they store beautifully in covered containers at a moderate room temperature.

These guidelines will help you develop a no-hassle routine for making all kinds of chocolate extravaganzas:

Divide the steps into utilitarian and artistic ones. Mold the containers one day, so that the bowl of tempered chocolate is dedicated to that single activity. Make the decorations another day, concentrating exclusively on those skills. Then, and this is the fun part, set aside another uninterrupted block of time to assemble all of the pieces—peacefully—without having to worry about doing a dozen other things at the same time.

Work in a cool room. Many of these pieces require extra handling, so touching the chocolate with warm hands is apt to blemish the surface. Chocolate twigs and bark, which are made of very thin layers of chocolate, are especially susceptible. Running an electric fan and wearing cotton gloves (see page 13) will help minimize unsightly surface fingerprints, as will buffing the chocolate with a soft brush (see page 15).

Always assume that someone will eat whatever you make in chocolate. Don't decorate your work with anything inedible.

Chocolate Woven Heart Basket with Sculpted Chocolate Roses

This lovely little basket is a perfect hostess gift to fill with your own homemade truffles or with specialties from your local candy shop. There's nothing wrong with combining your artistic efforts with somebody else's candy—provided the quality of both is comparable. Besides, doing so will give you more time to be creative.

All chocolate baskets begin with a molded base embedded with edible posts. Cake pans make perfect molds because they come in many shapes and sizes. Plastic storage food containers and empty ice cream or whipped-topping containers work well, too.

The edible posts should be the appropriate thickness and height for the size of the basket. I use full or half-size Bodgon's Candy Reception Sticks or pretzels for most baskets this size (see Notes).

For baskets up to 9 inches in diameter, the rolled chocolate-clay ropes should be slightly less than ½ inch thick. The smaller the basket, the thinner the rope should be. Always begin and end the weaving behind a post (on the inside of the basket) to conceal the seams.

Red and green food coloring

Milk Chocolate Clay (page 77)

1 ½ pounds semisweet chocolate, coarsely chopped, plus 6 ounces semisweet chocolate, in chunks (for tempering)

16 Bogdon's Candy Reception Sticks, cut in half, or pretzels (see Notes)

Dark Chocolate Clay (page 77)

Several Chocolate Spaghetti Twigs (page 89), optional

1. Clear a 3-foot-wide area of smooth work surface. Using the food coloring, dye four-fifths of the milk chocolate clay red and one-fifth green. With the red clay, make an assortment of roses and rosebuds (see page 78), and with the green clay, several 1-inch-long leaves (see page 83). Have at hand a sheet of waxed paper, a pair of wire clippers, a parchment decorating bag, a watercolor brush, and one 9-inch heart-shaped cake pan.

2. Melt and temper 1¼ pounds of the chopped semisweet chocolate (see page 22). Set aside ¼ cup of chocolate. Pour the rest into the cake pan, spreading it evenly with a rubber spatula. Tap the bottom of the mold on the work surface. Embed 31 reception sticks in the wet chocolate (flat-side-in), leaning them against the side of the mold at 1-inch intervals. Using an odd number will assure that the ropes will wrap around alternate posts in each row. Don't move the mold until the chocolate begins to set along the edges, or the sticks may topple over like dominoes. If they do, fish them out of the wet chocolate and re-embed them. Using the brush and the reserved chocolate, coat the bare parts on the sticks as you go along. Refrigerate until set, about 20 minutes.

3. Invert the mold onto the waxed paper, flexing the sides to release the chocolate. Turn the chocolate base upright.

4. Using the heel of your hand, knead a handful of firm semisweet chocolate clay on the work surface until it is the consistency of Play-Doh: soft and malleable, but not sticky. Using your fingertips, roll and stretch it into a rope slightly less than ½ inch thick.

5. To weave the basket: Begin in the center of the heart. Press the end of the rope against the chocolate base, directly behind the first candy post. Weave it in between the other posts, keeping the rope fairly taut. End each rope behind a post, cutting it there if necessary. Knead more clay and roll another rope, butting it against the first one by pressing gently. Weave 3 more rows, ending where the weaving began. Snip the tops of the posts with wire clippers to make them even with the ropes. Knead more clay and roll two 31-inch-long ropes, laying them side by side. Twist them into a braid.

6. Melt the rest of the chopped chocolate, using a leftover chunk to temper it. Spoon it into a parchment bag, cutting a ¼-inch opening in the tip. To attach the braid, pipe a small dollop of chocolate on each post. Lay the braid across the top of the basket, beginning and ending in the center. Press gently to secure it, joining the 2 ends with more chocolate.

7. Attach the clay roses, leaves, and spaghetti twigs (if using) to the upper right edge of the heart with piped dollops of chocolate. Air-dry the basket thoroughly before storing it in an airtight container at a moderate room temperature for 1 year or more. Store the leftover chocolate from the parchment bag at room temperature for future use.

> Makes one 9-inch heart-shaped basket

Chocolate Notes

Bogdon's Candy Reception Sticks are sold in candy shops all over the country and through mail-order catalogs (see page 152). You can substitute small pretzel sticks, which you must first dip in chocolate.

Reception sticks are fragile, especially if overchilled. If one should break, fasten it to the base with a small piece of chocolate clay and weave the ropes around it carefully.

Chocolate Twig Basket

This rustic chocolate twig basket begs to be filled with goodies that reflect nature's landscape: nuts, cocoa-dusted truffles, pecan-encrusted toffee, dipped glacé fruit, or something as simple as chocolate chip cookies.

The basket is made up of two parts: a molded shell surrounded by a stockade of chocolate twigs. Select a container with straight sides measuring about 2 ½ inches high, such as a quart-size empty plastic ice cream container. If there are ridges at the top of the container, cut them off with a pair of sharp scissors so that they don't inhibit the release of the chocolate.

When chocolate is spread on a cool surface, it dries gradually. During each drying stage, it is capable of only doing certain things, so you must be patient as you wait for it to reach the right degree of dryness. It takes a drier chocolate to make chocolate twigs than it does to make tree bark (see page 85) or striped bands (see page 114). The only way to know if it's ready is to test it with a wall scraper.

Handle the twigs with cotton gloves (see page 13), or your fingerprints will cause a white spot to appear on the surface.

2 pounds semisweet chocolate, coarsely chopped, plus 4 ounces semisweet chocolate, in chunks (for tempering)

1. Melt and temper half of the chopped chocolate (see page 22). Using a 2 ½-by-5-inch ice cream container as a mold, make a hollow chocolate basket (see page 65).

2. Clear a 3-foot-wide area of work surface. If you have a marble slab, place it in front of you, with the longest side parallel with the edge of the work surface. Otherwise, select an alternative work surface (see page 14), cleaning and drying it thoroughly. Line a large rimless baking sheet with waxed paper, securing it with tape. Line a pattern board with waxed paper (see page 15). Have at hand an angled metal spatula, 3- and 6-inch wall scrapers, a parchment decorating bag, a white cotton glove, and a 3 ½-foot-long piece of ribbon.

3. Melt the remaining chopped chocolate along with the leftover chocolate from the molding procedure, tempering it with the same chunks as before. When not in use, keep the bowl of chocolate in a pan or a slightly larger bowl of warm (90°F) water, replenishing the warm water as needed. Stir the chocolate occasionally, scraping the sides of the bowl. Dry the bottom of the bowl each time you remove it from the water.

4. Pour ½ cup chocolate in the center of the marble or work surface. Spread it horizontally with the angled spatula and then vertically with the 6-inch wall scraper until it is slightly less than $1/16$ inch thick.

5. Let set until the chocolate feels dry and no longer smudges when you touch it. Now, begin testing the perimeter with the 3-inch wall scraper. Holding the handle, palm down, at a 30-degree angle to the surface, push the blade forward. It will roll into a tight curl if it's ready. If it isn't, wait and try again. You cannot hurry the drying process.

6. Beginning in the lower right-hand corner, push the scraper forward about 5 inches, making a tightly curled "twig" about $1/16$ inch in diameter. (Use the opposite side if you're left-handed.) Slide the blade under the twig to lift and transfer it to the baking sheet. Repeat until you run out of chocolate to scrape or until the chocolate splinters into shreds. Scrape the surface clean, reserving the leftovers for future use. Pour more melted chocolate and repeat the process until you have about 45 twigs.

7. Place the molded container on the pattern board. Spoon the left-over chocolate into the parchment bag and cut a $1/4$-inch opening in the tip. Using a gloved hand, attach a stockade of twigs around the outside of the basket, affixing them with piped vertical lines of chocolate. Let set. Wrap a ribbon around the sides of the basket and fill it with cocoa-dusted truffles, nuts, or toffee, or store the empty basket in an airtight container at a moderate room temperature for up to 1 year.

8. Refrigerate the leftover chocolate on a sheet of waxed paper until set and store, along with the other leftovers, in an airtight container at a moderate room temperature for future use.

> Makes one 5½-inch round basket

VARIATION:

Chocolate Twig Basket Cake: Press a stockade of chocolate twigs around the sides of a whipped cream–coated cake for an easy decoration. Pile juicy red berries on top and wrap the sides with a bright red ribbon.

Chocolate Bowl with Grape Clusters

You can make this festive holiday centerpiece in stages, months before the first snowflakes begin to fall. Since the grape clusters are piped on waxed paper, you have plenty of time to practice and improve your chocolate "beading" skills (see page 75) before you attach them to the bowl.

1 ounce Milk Chocolate Clay (page 77)

4 ounces milk chocolate, coarsely chopped, plus one 1-ounce chunk milk chocolate (for tempering)

One 9¾-inch molded semisweet chocolate bowl (see page 62)

Chocolate-dipped glacé fruit, cookies, or Rich Chocolate Mousse (page 138) for serving

1. Clear a 3-foot-wide area of smooth work surface. Have at hand 2 waxed paper–lined pattern boards (see page 15), a rolling pin, a small leaf cutter or sharp craft knife, a toothpick, a parchment decorating bag, and an angled metal spatula.

2. Using the heel of your hand, knead the chocolate clay on the work surface until it is the consistency of Play-Doh: soft and malleable, but not sticky. With the rolling pin, flatten it on the pattern board into a thin sheet. Using the leaf cutter or a knife, make 30 small leaves, each about ½ inch long, marking the veins with a toothpick.

3. Melt and temper the chopped chocolate (see page 22). Spoon it into the parchment bag, cutting a ⅛-inch opening in the tip. To pipe the 20 grape clusters, hold the bag at a 45-degree angle to the other pattern board. Pipe a 1-inch-long outline of a grape cluster. Starting at the tip and continuing down both sides, squeeze out bead-shaped grapes. Fill in the center with more beads. Let set. Then pipe a few more beads on top of each cluster.

4. Place the chocolate bowl on a decorator's turntable (or on a tall box) and work on it from a sitting position. Using the same parchment bag, pipe a curving vine all the way around the bowl, about ½ inch from the top. Pipe short branches in the curves for the grape clusters and leaves, attaching them with piped dots of chocolate. Pipe spiral tendrils at random intervals.

5. Use now, or store the empty chocolate bowl in an airtight container at room temperature for up to 1 year.

6. Refrigerate the leftover chocolate on a sheet of waxed paper until set and store in an airtight container at room temperature for future use.

7. Fill the bowl with dipped glacé fruit, cookies, or chocolate mousse.

Makes one 9¾-inch bowl

Chocolate Note

To make a chocolate bowl on a pedestal, use 2 pounds of chocolate and 8 ounces of chunks. After molding the bowl, fill a 4- or 5-by-1½-inch plastic or metal bowl to the rim with some of the leftover chocolate. Tap the back of the mold on the work surface and refrigerate for about 20 minutes. Release it from the mold and let sit at a moderate room temperature at least 15 minutes before attaching it to the chocolate bowl with a dollop of tempered chocolate.

Embroidered Chocolate Box

Real embroidery bears little resemblance to brush embroidery, which is a cake-decorating technique that I adapted for chocolate work. It requires no cake-decorating expertise and, when combined with another technique called "etching," it enables an inexperienced decorator to pipe designs on chocolate like an expert.

The process begins by drawing a simple design on paper that will fit the 6-inch diameter of the candy box lid. Making a separate pattern for the sides of the box is optional.

Next, the design is etched onto the chocolate surface through the paper with a sharp-pointed tool like a scriber or a nail (see page 15). When it's time to decorate the box, the chocolate is piped directly over the etched lines, eliminating the fear of doing it freehand.

The piped lines are brushed before they dry, making them look as if they've been embroidered on the surface of the chocolate. A light dusting of gold powder adds a luxurious finishing touch.

One 6-inch round white chocolate lid
(see page 65)

One 6-inch round white chocolate
hollow box (see page 65)

4 ounces milk chocolate, coarsely chopped,
plus one 1-ounce chunk milk chocolate
(for tempering)

3 tiny gold dragées

Super Gold Luster Dust (see page 14)

1. Clear a 3-foot-wide area of work surface. Line a pattern board with waxed paper (see page 15). Have at hand a 6-inch round cake pan, 2 sheets of lightweight paper, a sharp-pointed tool (see recipe introduction), a parchment decorating bag, 2 No. 000 artists' brushes, and a pair of tweezers.

2. Trace the bottom of the cake pan on a sheet of paper and cut it out. Draw or trace a design on the paper as you want it to appear on the chocolate lid. Draw another pattern for the sides of the bottom of the box, if you think you need it. Place the chocolate lid on a lined pattern board, face up, covering it with the pattern. Using the pointed tool, press over the lines to etch the design onto the chocolate without tearing the paper. Remove the paper.

3. Melt and temper the chopped chocolate (see page 22). Spoon it into the parchment bag and cut a 1/16-inch opening in the tip.

4. Following the etched pattern, pipe the outline of one petal at a time, stopping in between to stroke the brush through the wet line of chocolate toward the center of the petal, filling in most of that area. Clean the brush frequently, removing the excess chocolate. Using the tweezers, immediately stud the center of the large flower with the dragées. Pipe and brush the other flowers.

5. Pipe the stems and leaves. Brush the leaves outwardly from the center vein, through the outside line, creating ragged edges. Clean the brush before drawing it across the center of each leaf to form the vein. Pipe the stems and leaves on the sides of the box, repeating the brush strokes as directed. Refrigerate until set, about 5 minutes.

6. Lightly touch the surface of the gold luster dust with the other brush, tapping the excess into the lid of its container. Brush it on the petals and leaves.

7. Use the box at once, or store in an airtight container at room temperature for up to 8 months.

8. Store the leftover chocolate from the parchment bag in an airtight container at room temperature for future use.

Makes one 6-inch round box with a lid

Mexican Chocolate Box

I spend a lot of time in Oaxaca, Mexico, partly because of its rich choco-late heritage, but also because I love it there. The Oaxaqueños, who are masters of folk art, are famous for their hammered tin boxes painted in bright, sunny colors. My chocolate version is decorated with confec-tionery-coating clay decorations that I cut out with cookie cutters and/or a sharp craft knife. Whether you use this design or one of your own, cre-ating a similar box would be a delightful family activity.

2 pounds semisweet chocolate, coarsely chopped, plus 8 ounces semisweet chocolate, in chunks (for tempering)

10 ounces White Confectionery Coating Clay (page 77)

Yellow, red, purple, blue, and green food coloring

1. Clear a 4-foot-wide area of smooth work surface. Line 5 pattern boards with waxed paper (see page 15), or line 2 large rimless baking sheets with waxed paper, securing it with tape. Have at hand about 6 toothpicks, a rolling pin, a flower-shaped cookie cutter, a No. 1A decorating tip, a craft-type knife, and two 8-by-2-inch straight-sided round cake pans.

2. Melt and temper the chopped chocolate (see page 22). Using the 8-inch cake pans, mold a hollow box and lid (see page 65). It will take about 1½ cups chocolate to mold the bottom of the box and slightly less than ¾ cup for the lid. Spread the leftover chocolate on a sheet of waxed paper, refrigerate until set, and store in an airtight container at a moderate room temperature for future use.

3. Divide the clay into 5 pieces (2 ounces each). Using a different toothpick to apply each color, dye the pieces yellow, red, purple, blue, and green with food coloring (see page 13).

4. Using a rolling pin, flatten each piece of clay into a thin strip on a separate pattern board or on the 2 baking sheets. Lift the strips on and off the paper to prevent sticking. Using the cutters and/or the knife, cut out 3 red, 3 purple, 3 blue, and 3 green flowers, twelve ½-inch-diameter yellow circles, a multicolored bird, and about sixty-five ½-inch-long leaves in assorted colors.

5. Immediately press the pieces against the lid and sides of the box. Using a clean toothpick, define the veins on the leaves, the lines on the flowers, and the feathers on the bird.

6. Use the box at once, or air-dry thoroughly and store in an airtight container at room temperature for up to 1 year.

Makes one 8-inch round box with a lid

Marbleized Egg on a Pedestal

After watching house painters apply faux-marble finishes to walls with a sponge and a bucket of paint, I began using a similar technique with chocolate. At first, I used a sponge too, but one day when I found myself without one, I substituted a wad of waxed paper. To my surprise, the paper worked so well that I never went back to using a sponge.

Use a waxed paper–covered pattern board (see page 15) or a small baking sheet as a "palette." Place a dollop of chocolate off to one side, leaving room to blot the excess chocolate before dabbing it inside the mold.

To achieve a marbled effect, apply the darkest color first, followed by 2 or 3 progressively lighter shades—always leaving some part of the cavity walls bare for the chocolate shell to show through.

To avoid disappointing results, never combine layers of colored confectionery coating with layers of real chocolate, because the fats are incompatible. Doing so would cause the chocolate to "bloom."

1 ounce Milk Chocolate Clay (page 77)

2 ounces Dark Chocolate Clay (page 77)

2 ounces semisweet chocolate, coarsely chopped

1 pound white chocolate couverture, coarsely chopped, plus 4 ounces white chocolate couverture, in chunks (for tempering)

6 ounces milk chocolate, coarsely chopped, plus one 1½-ounce chunk milk chocolate (for tempering)

Super Gold Luster Dust (see page 14)

¼ teaspoon vodka or other white spirits

1. Clear a 3-foot-wide area of work surface. Line 2 pattern boards with waxed paper (see page 15). Have at hand an angled metal spatula, a sheet of waxed paper, a dampened reusable cleaning cloth, a small baking sheet, a craft knife, a rolling pin, a parchment decorating bag, 2 No. 000 artists' brushes, two 5½-by-3¾-inch hollow egg molds (see Note), and one 3-by-1-inch round plastic dish (see Note).

2. Using the milk chocolate clay, make 3 small roses (see page 78). Using a rolling pin, flatten the dark chocolate clay into a thin strip on a pattern board. Lift it on and off to prevent sticking. Using a leaf cutter and a knife, cut out 6 to 8 leaves (see page 83) and twelve ½-by-2½-inch-long strips. Pinch the ends of 4 strips to form loops. Cut the remaining strips diagonally at one end to form the ends of the ribbons.

3. Melt the semisweet chocolate and pour it onto the pattern board. Temper it by paddling it with the angled spatula until it feels cool (see page 24). Scrunch the waxed paper in your hand, forming a wad with an irregular surface. Rub it in the chocolate, blot the excess, and dab it in a random pattern on the inside of each egg cavity. Keep moistening the wad with more chocolate as needed. Let the molds sit.

4. Melt and temper the chopped white and milk chocolates (see page 22). Place the bowl of white chocolate in a pan or a slightly larger bowl of warm (88°F) water, replenishing the warm water as needed. Stir the chocolate occasionally, scraping the sides of the bowl. Dry the bottom of the bowl each time you remove it from the water. Using the same wad of paper and about 3 tablespoons of milk chocolate, rub, blot, and dab it in the cavities, leaving parts of the surface bare. (It's okay if the first layer is still wet.) Discard the wad. Pour the leftover milk chocolate in the small dish, tap the bottom on the work surface, and refrigerate until set, about 15 minutes.

5. Using the white chocolate, mold the egg halves (see page 62). Refrigerate until set, about 15 minutes. Invert the molds onto the waxed paper to release them. If the leftover chocolate starts to thicken, place it over a pan of hot water for a few seconds or microwave on low (30 percent) power in 10-second increments, never letting the temperature of the chocolate exceed 88°F.

6. Warm the small baking sheet in a 200°F oven. Using gloved hands, invert the 2 molded shells onto the baking sheet. Rub the shells around in circles for about 3 seconds, slightly melting the edges. Immediately align the 2 wet edges, pressing them together firmly. Wipe the seam and let set for about 5 minutes. Wash and rewarm the baking sheet. Stand the egg upright on the warm baking sheet this time, rubbing it in circles to flatten the bottom.

7. Spoon the leftover white chocolate into a parchment decorating bag, cutting a ¼-inch opening in the tip. Attach the egg to the pedestal and the ribbons and roses to the top with piped dollops of chocolate. Add the loops and leaves with more chocolate.

8. Lightly touch the surface of the gold luster dust with one of the artists' brushes, tapping the excess into the lid of its container. Brush highlights on the edges of the rose petals and leaves. Using another brush, dampened with vodka or other spirits, paint a few thin gold veins in a random pattern on the surface of the egg.

Makes one 8-by-3¼-inch egg on a pedestal

Chocolate Note
Since egg mold sizes vary so much, be prepared to use a little more (or less) chocolate than specified. For the egg pedestal mold, consider using a 3¼-inch round plastic take-out container from a restaurant.

Chocolate Driftwood Centerpiece

I originally designed this centerpiece to commemorate Nestlé's celebration of the invention of milk chocolate by Daniel Peter, using his friend Henri Nestlé's condensed milk. To honor Daniel Peter, the Nestlé Food Company calls its industrial chocolate division Peter's Chocolate. The little nest, which is similar to the one that identifies their company, can be used to express many sentiments.

Make each of the components ahead of time. You'll need 3 chocolate clay roses, 6 rosebuds, six 1½-inch-long leaves, a nest with 3 birds, about 20 "berries," 12 to 15 pieces of bark, and an 11-by-7-inch molded oval chocolate plate.

When it's time to assemble the sculpture, spread everything out before you. With gloved hands, practice arranging the bark pieces in different combinations on the lined baking sheet. Then assemble them, using balls of clay and small bottles to prop up the branches while the chocolate "glue" is drying.

Express yourself artistically by adding other decorative touches with or without the bird's nest. The sculpture is equally beautiful when it's decorated with a simple floral arrangement.

> 6 ounces Dark Chocolate Clay (page 77)
>
> 1 ounce Milk Chocolate Clay (page 77)
>
> 1 ounce White Confectionery Coating Clay (page 77)
>
> 2 pounds milk chocolate, coarsely chopped, plus 8 ounces milk chocolate, in chunks (for tempering)
>
> Several Chocolate Spaghetti Twigs (page 89), optional

1. Clear a 3-foot-wide area of work surface. Line a large rimless baking sheet with waxed paper, securing it with tape. Line a pattern board with waxed paper (see page 15). If you have a marble slab, place it in front of you, with the longest side parallel to the edge of the work surface. Otherwise, select an alternative work surface (see page 14), cleaning and drying it thoroughly. Have at hand an angled metal spatula, a 6-inch wall scraper, a parchment decorating bag, white cotton gloves (see page 13), a small pair of pointed scissors, a pasta machine (see Note), and one 11-by-7-inch oval metal or plastic tray.

2. Using the heel of your hand, knead the dark chocolate clay on the work surface until it is the consistency of Play-Doh: soft and malleable, but not sticky. Make 2 small roses, 3 rosebuds (see page 78), and 6 leaves (see page 83). Flatten 1 ounce of the clay between your fingers to a thickness of ¼ inch. Feed it through the rollers of a pasta machine set on No. 1, usually the widest opening, while cranking the handle. Repeat 3 or 4 more times, tightening the rollers a notch each time, finishing with setting No. 4 or 5. Remove the handle and reposition it opposite the spaghetti-cutting blades, with the pattern board underneath to catch the chocolate. Feed the thin strip through the cutting blades. Gather up the pile of spaghettilike strands with your thumbs and fingers, pressing gently to form a nest about 2½ inches in diameter.

3. Knead the milk chocolate and white confectionery coating clays separately. Using the milk chocolate clay, make 1 small mother bird and 2 smaller baby birds (see page 124). Using dots of red and orange food coloring applied with a toothpick, dye the white clay reddish orange. Use it to make about 20 tiny round "berries."

4. Melt and temper the chopped milk chocolate (see page 22). Mold the oval plate with half the chocolate (see page 59). When not in use, keep the bowl of the remaining chocolate in a pan or a larger bowl of warm (88°F) water, replenishing the warm

water as needed. Stir the chocolate occasionally, scraping the sides of the bowl. Dry the bottom of the bowl before pouring from it. Using the wall scraper, make about 20 pieces of tree bark (see page 85), which includes several extra pieces. Let set on the baking sheet at a moderate room temperature, first bending some slightly while they're still malleable.

5. Attach the chocolate plate to a slightly smaller corrugated cake cardboard with a dab of chocolate. Spoon the remaining chocolate into the parchment bag, cutting a ¼-inch opening in the tip. Attach 2 curved pieces of bark at the back of the plate with piped lines of chocolate, forming an arc. Attach additional pieces to the top or sides of the arc to thicken its girth so that it resembles a piece of driftwood. Attach 2 standing curved "branches" of bark in the center of the log with dollops of chocolate and prop them from behind with balls of clay or small bottles until the chocolate sets. Attach the nest, birds, roses, rosebuds, leaves, spaghetti twigs (optional), and "berries" with more chocolate.

| Makes one 11-by-7-inch oval centerpiece |

Chocolate Note

If you don't have a pasta machine, use a rolling pin and a knife to flatten and cut the chocolate clay into thin spaghettilike strands to make the bird's nest.

spectacular chocolate cakes and desserts

As a chocolate artist, I take special pleasure in presenting cakes that feature spectacular chocolate decorations. This glorious array of cakes and desserts showcases some of chocolate's extraordinary versatility.

While fancy decorated cakes like these always require a little extra effort, many of their components, including the decorations, can be made ahead of time. The basic cakes, fillings, frostings, and sauces used in many of these spectacular creations are found in the last chapter of this book. All of the cakes freeze beautifully, and the fillings and frostings can be made a day or two (or more) in advance. I always like to get the preliminary work out of the way so that I can concentrate on the part I love best: adding the finishing touches.

It won't take long for you to begin stockpiling a supply of leftover clay, molded chocolate leaves, and other odds and ends from earlier projects. If you have the space, you can make almost all of the decorations in this book days, weeks, or months in advance, and then store them at room temperature until you need them. That is one of the benefits of working with tempered chocolate. You do not have that option when you work with untempered chocolate. Decorations made with *untempered* chocolate must be kept refrigerated until just before serving. If they are left at room temperature, they will discolor, soften, and become increasingly unappealing as time passes.

These simple steps will show you the professional way to cut, fill, reassemble, and frost your cake layers in advance, in preparation for the spectacular decorations that await them.

CUTTING A CAKE INTO LAYERS

1. Line a work surface with waxed paper. First place the cake, top-side-down, on a slightly smaller corrugated cake circle; then place it on a decorator's turntable or directly on the work surface.

2. To cut a cake into 2 layers, position the blade of a long serrated knife midway up the side of the cake, parallel to the turntable. Place your hand, palm down, on the top of the cake, turning the cake counterclockwise as you make a shallow cut all the way around the side, marking the split between the layers. Make progressively deeper cuts into the cake until the knife penetrates the center and passes through to the other side.

3. Slide another corrugated cake circle, the removable bottom of a quiche pan, or rimless baking sheet between the layers to lift and remove the top layer.

FILLING A CAKE AND REASSEMBLING THE LAYERS

1. For cakes with thick fillings, fit a 10-inch pastry bag with an open coupler (see page 13) and fill it half full of frosting. Do not attach the coupler ring. Pipe a thick band of frosting around the top edge of the cake to contain the filling. Using an angled metal spatula, spread the filling across the center. For thin layers of filling, omit the border of frosting and spread a ⅛- to ¼-inch-thick layer of filling to within ¼ inch of the edge.

❧ Enchanted Forest Cake, page 118.

2. For a 2-layer cake, coax the top layer to hang slightly over the edge of the cake circle or whatever is supporting it. Place the second layer on top of the filling, aligning the edges of both layers as you slide the cardboard out from under the top one. For a multilayer cake, fill and layer the remaining layers the same way, placing the top layer bottom-side-up.

COVERING A CAKE WITH BUTTERCREAM

1. Place the cake on a decorator's turntable or on a serving plate protected with several 3-inch-wide strips of waxed paper. The frosting should be soft and creamy, to avoid tearing the cake. To soften it, add 1 to 2 teaspoons of light corn syrup at a time, beating well after each addition.

2. Using a large metal spatula, place a mound of buttercream on top of the cake. Spread a thin, transparent coating across the top, pushing the excess down onto the sides of the cake. To avoid mixing crumbs into the frosting, don't allow the spatula to touch the bare cake, but always keep it submerged in the frosting. Cover the sides as well as the space between the layers with the excess frosting from the top, adding more if necessary. Holding the blade upright against the side of the cake, turn the turntable (or the serving plate) slowly, all the way around, without lifting the spatula. Remove the excess frosting, returning it to the bowl only if it is crumb free. This is only a "crumb coat," a transparent undercoat that is used to prime the cake before a second, heavier coating of frosting is applied. Refrigerate the cake for 15 minutes.

3. Using firm pressure and side-to-side movements, apply a thicker layer of buttercream over the top and sides of the cake, removing the excess with the spatula. To

❧ Spreading the "crumb coat."

smooth the sides, dip the spatula into hot water, shaking off the excess moisture. Holding the blade upright against the side of the cake, rotate the turntable slowly again, without lifting the spatula. Remove the excess frosting, returning it to the bowl only if it is crumb free. To smooth the top, dip the spatula in hot water and remove the excess moisture with a paper towel. Hold the flat blade of the spatula against the top of the cake with the end touching the center of the cake. Rotate the turntable counterclockwise. Remove the excess frosting with the metal spatula.

COVERING A CAKE WITH WHIPPED CREAM

Proceed as directed above except for the final step. To smooth the surface, use as few spatula strokes as possible, since overworking the cream will cause its texture to become dry and porous.

COVERING A CAKE WITH CHOCOLATE GLAZE

1. Prepare the glaze (see page 144) and let cool to a fudgy consistency, about 1 hour.

2. Examine the top of the cake to be sure the edges are level with the center. If not, press them down firmly with your fingertips or trim them with a serrated knife. Cover the cake with a slightly smaller corrugated cake circle, inverting it so that the bottom of the cake is now the top. Place the cake on a decorator's turntable or on a wire cake rack set over a large baking sheet.

3. Using a metal spatula, place ½ cup of thick glaze on top of the cake. Spread a thin layer over all of the cake, adding more if necessary. Let this "crumb coat" set to form a light crust, about 30 minutes.

4. Place the bowl of glaze over a pan of hot water without allowing the two containers to touch. Stir gently, until the glaze reaches 90° to 95°F and has the consistency of heavy cream. Remove the bowl from the heat.

5. Wipe the bottom of the bowl and pour the glaze through a sieve directly onto the center of the top of the cake. Using a clean, dry large metal spatula and as few strokes as possible, spread the glaze over the top, coaxing it to run over the sides of the cake while rotating the turntable/baking sheet. Jiggle the turntable gently to level the glaze. Touch up the sides with the metal spatula, but avoid fussing with the top. Slide a large spatula under the cake to lift and transfer it to a clean wire cake rack. Let the glaze set for about 30 minutes.

❧ Pouring the glaze through a sieve onto the cake.

❧ Spreading the glaze over the cake.

❧ Jiggling the turntable to level the glaze.

Chocolate Swiss-Cheese Cake

This cake uses one of my favorite materials: white chocolate "Swiss cheese." Cutting the holes in the "cheese" is fun, provided you do so before the chocolate sets completely; otherwise, the pieces may splinter. Generally, the cooler the room, the faster you must work. If you feel up to the task, Mouse Truffles are the perfect accompaniments.

4 ounces white chocolate, coarsely chopped, plus one 1½-ounce chunk white chocolate (for tempering)

4 tablespoons unsweetened cocoa powder

Chocolate Cheesecake (page 129)

Mouse Truffles (page 46), optional

1. Draw or trace an 8-inch circle on a sheet of paper and cut it out. Line an evenly flat large rimless baking sheet with waxed paper, securing it with tape. Have at hand a single sheet of plastic cut from a 1-gallon-size plastic storage bag, an angled metal spatula, a craft-type knife with a thin blade, No. 1A and No. 12 decorating tips, and a small sieve.

2. Melt and temper the chopped white chocolate (see page 22). Pour the chocolate in a puddle onto the lined baking sheet. With an angled metal spatula, spread it evenly into a 9-inch square or circle. Rap the bottom of the baking sheet on the work surface to smooth the chocolate. Refrigerate until the chocolate is *barely* set, about 5 minutes.

3. Using the craft-type knife with the paper circle as a pattern, cut out an 8-inch circle of white chocolate. Fold the paper in half. Using the straight edge of the paper as a guide, cut the chocolate circle in half horizontally and vertically, then cut each of the quarters into 3 triangles. Using the small openings of both decorating tips, immediately cut large and small holes in each triangle before the chocolate sets completely. Next, quickly slide the angled metal spatula under the triangles to release them from the waxed paper. You must release the chocolate from the waxed paper as soon as it sets, or the edges will curl and the pieces will not lie flat on the cake.

4. Sift the cocoa directly over the surface of the cheesecake. Arrange 12 "Swiss cheese" triangles on top, spaced evenly apart, with the points barely meeting in the center. Arrange 2 or 3 Mouse Truffles on top, if using, or serve 1 Mouse Truffle alongside a pool of Razzberry Sauce (page 142) with each serving.

Makes one 9-inch round cheesecake; serves 10 to 12

Berry Basket Cake

Seasonal berries share center stage with chocolate in this eye-catching party cake. The paper-thin band of chocolate that surrounds the cake is made on a long strip of acetate or polycoated freezer paper, using a simple molding technique with many variations (see page 71). Since cakes often vary in height, always measure the sides of any cake that is to be banded before you cut the strip. This band should be slightly taller than the height of the cake in order to contain and support the pile of berries.

Brown Velvet Glaze (page 144)

2 tablespoons seedless raspberry jelly

Dee's Super-Moist Cake (page 131)

2 ounces white chocolate,
   coarsely chopped, plus one ½-ounce
   chunk white chocolate (for tempering)

4 ounces semisweet chocolate, coarsely
   chopped, plus one 1-ounce chunk
   semisweet chocolate (for tempering)

2 pints assorted fresh berries
   (hulled strawberries, red and black
   raspberries, and blueberries)

2 or 3 fresh mint leaves (optional)

1. Prepare the glaze and let cool to 90° to 95°F, about 30 minutes. In a small saucepan, heat the jelly until melted, stirring frequently. Let cool completely.

2. If necessary, trim the sides of the cake with a serrated knife, making them symmetrical, to allow the chocolate band to hug them properly. If the corrugated cake circle shows under the cake, trim it with sharp scissors. Have at hand a small pair of scissors, a parchment decorating bag, a long metal spatula, a small pastry brush, and one 26-by-2¼-inch strip of acetate or polycoated freezer paper (see page 12). Glaze the cake without applying a "crumb coat" (see page 109).

3. Clear a 3-foot-wide area of work surface and line it with a 30-inch-long sheet of waxed paper. Lay the acetate or freezer-paper strip across it. (Lay freezer paper shiny-side-up.)

4. Melt and temper both chocolates (see page 22). Place the bowl of semisweet chocolate in a pan or slightly larger bowl of warm (90°F) water, replenishing the warm water as needed. Stir the chocolate occasionally, scraping the sides of the bowl.

5. Spoon the white chocolate into the parchment bag, cutting a ¼-inch opening in the tip. Holding the bag about 5 inches above the surface, pipe a random pattern of scribbly lines across the length of the strip, extending them beyond the edges. Lift the strip and set it aside until the chocolate lines set, about 3 to 5 minutes. Replace the chocolate-coated paper on the work surface with a fresh sheet. (When the chocolate hardens, it is reusable.)

6. Place the piped strip back on the waxed paper. Dry the bottom of the bowl containing the dark chocolate and pour a ½-inch-wide line of it across the length of the strip. Using an angled metal spatula, spread it in a thin, even layer across the strip, extending it beyond the edges. Lift the strip by one corner. Rub your fingertips along both edges, removing the surplus chocolate. Let the strip sit for about 1 minute.

7. Slide the long spatula under the cake and transfer it to a decorator's turntable or a serving platter. Pick up the ends of the strip with both hands. Place the center of the strip against the back wall of the cake, with the chocolate side facing in. Bring the ends toward you, wrapping the strip snugly around both sides of the cake at one time. Press one end flat against the side of the cake. Using scissors, cut the other end so that both ends butt up

evenly without overlapping. Refrigerate until the chocolate band is completely set, about 15 minutes.

8. To complete the cake, slice the strawberries in half lengthwise (or in thirds if the berries are large). Arrange an assortment of berries on top, along with the mint leaves, if using. Using a small pastry brush, glaze the strawberries with the jam. Refrigerate again for about 5 minutes. Release a corner of the strip and peel it off carefully, leaving the chocolate band attached to the sides of the cake.

9. Store all the leftover chocolate in an airtight container at room temperature for future use.

Makes one 8-inch, single-layer round cake; serves 8 to 10

Chocolate Note

Chocolate takes longer to set on acetate strips than it does on freezer paper, but it produces a much higher shine. The chocolate will *not* shine, however, if you release it too soon. Wait until the plastic has a frosted appearance.

Chocolate Banana Cream Cake

Bananas and cream are a winning combination in this scrumptious rum-spiked chocolate sponge cake. The wavy striped chocolate bands are fun to make using an adhesive spreader (see page 15) and two wall scrapers with 3- and 6-inch wide blades (page 15). Though marble and granite are the preferred surfaces to use for this project, Corian, Formica, and metal are also acceptable. Wood or grouted ceramic tile surfaces are not recommended. As with all techniques of this kind, it is important to work in a cool (65° to 70°F) room—unless you are blessed with the patience of a saint.

All of the components of this cake, including the wavy chocolate bands, can be made in advance and assembled several hours to 1 day ahead. The cake actually improves in taste and texture as it waits to be served.

Chocolate Sponge Cake (page 133)

¼ cup rum-flavored Simple Syrup (page 142)

⅔ cup strained apricot preserves

Chocolate Pastry Cream (page 141)

Four 6-inch-long bananas,
    peeled and cut crosswise into ¼-inch slices

Whipped Cream (page 139)

8 ounces white chocolate, coarsely
    chopped, plus one 2-ounce chunk white
    chocolate (for tempering)

8 ounces semisweet or milk chocolate,
    coarsely chopped, plus one 2-ounce chunk
    semisweet or milk chocolate (for
    tempering)

1. Clear a 3-foot-wide area of work surface and line it with waxed paper. Place the sponge cake, top-side-down, on a slightly smaller corrugated cake circle. Cut it horizontally into 3 layers (see page 107). Using a corrugated cake circle or the removable bottom of a quiche pan, lift and move the 2 top layers to the paper-lined work surface. Using a pastry brush, moisten the bottom layer with half the simple syrup. Spread it with half the preserves, half the pastry cream, and a layer of half the bananas. Slide the other 2 stacked layers on top of the filled layer, aligning the sides symmetrically. Lift and remove the top layer. Spread the middle layer with the remaining preserves, pastry cream, and bananas. Place the final layer on top, moistening it with the remaining syrup.

2. Place the cake on a decorator's turntable or on a serving dish protected with strips of waxed paper. "Crumb coat" and frost the cake with whipped cream (see page 108). Keep refrigerated.

3. Clear the work surface again. If you have a marble slab, place it in front of you, with the longest side parallel to the edge of the work surface. If you don't, select an alternative work surface, cleaning and drying it thoroughly. Line a large baking sheet with waxed paper. Wad 4 or 5 sheets of waxed paper. Have at hand a small angled spatula, 3- and 6-inch wall scrapers, a clean, dry pastry brush, and an adhesive spreader.

4. Melt and temper both chopped chocolates (see page 22). Place the white chocolate in a pan or a slightly larger bowl of warm (88°F) water, replenishing the warm water as needed. Stir the chocolate occasionally, scraping the sides of the bowl. Dry the bottom of the bowl each time you remove it from the water.

5. To make the striped bands: Pour about ½ cup semisweet chocolate onto a cool but not cold work surface. Using an angled spatula, spread the chocolate horizontally, forming a thin layer. Immediately spread it vertically with the 6-inch wall scraper using multiple downward strokes, creating a larger thin layer less than 1/16 inch thick.

6. Let set until the surface no longer looks wet. Grasp the adhesive spreader firmly with both hands, fingers on top and thumbs underneath. Position it at a 10-degree angle to the surface, in the lower right-hand corner of the chocolate. Push the spreader forward very firmly, from one end of the chocolate to the other, creating grooves that expose the marble surface. The grooves must expose the work surface in order to be effective. Otherwise, the second color will not show through properly. Repeat to make grooves across the entire chocolate surface, ignoring (but not discarding) the pile of chocolate curlicues that accumulate. With a dry pastry brush, clean the chocolate debris from the grooves.

7. Stir the white chocolate and dry the bottom of the bowl. Immediately pour an equal amount of white chocolate over the dark-chocolate-striped surface, spreading it horizontally and then vertically with the same wall scraper to cover the stripes and fill in the grooves. Add more chocolate if necessary.

8. Let set for 3 or 4 minutes or longer, depending on the temperature of the room. The chocolate is ready to use when its perimeter feels dry and your fingertip no longer smudges the surface when you touch it. Grasp the handle of the 3-inch wall scraper, palm up. Position the blade at a 5-degree angle to the surface, in the lower right-hand corner of the chocolate. Push the blade forward, sliding it *under* the chocolate to see if it is supple enough to pull away from the marble in one piece. If it is, proceed immediately; if it is not supple, wait until it is.

9. Push the scraper forward about 6 inches, sliding it under the chocolate while lifting and supporting the chocolate band with the other hand as the band pulls away from the marble. While the band is still supple, lay it on the baking sheet, striped-side-up, and prop it underneath with the wads of waxed paper to keep it from lying flat. Repeat to make more bands of chocolate until all the chocolate is used or it becomes too dry and brittle to continue.

10. Scrape the leftover chocolate off the work surface with a wall scraper and store it in an airtight container at room temperature for future use (see Note). If there is enough tempered chocolate to continue making more bands, do so; otherwise, add it to the leftovers.

11. Arrange a pile of 3 or 4 wavy bands of striped chocolate on the top of the cake. Scatter the leftover chocolate curlicues around the base of the cake if you like, or store them in an airtight container for future use.

> Makes one 9-inch, 3-layer round cake; serves 12

Chocolate Note
Mixtures of leftover dark and white chocolates (or milk chocolate) can be reused, in spite of the differences in color and composition. Blend small portions of it at a time into various batches of fresh dark chocolate, so as not to lighten its color.

Andalusian Torte

This cake evokes memories of the gardens of the Alhambra, where gardenias grow in great profusion. The petals of the gardenias on this cake, each modeled entirely by hand from confectionery clay, are much more lasting. I never tire of making confectionery flowers, and neither will you. Like all of the other components of this cake, they can be made in advance and plucked from storage at a moment's notice.

Brown Velvet Glaze (page 144)

Chocolate-Almond Torte (page 132)

2 Chocolate Clay Gardenias and 2 or 3 Chocolate Clay Gardenia Buds (page 82)

7 Chocolate Clay Leaves (see page 83)

1. Prepare the glaze. Use it to "crumb coat" and glaze the cake (see page 109), reserving the remaining glaze. Let set for 30 minutes before decorating. Cut a parchment triangle in half, rolling one piece into a decorating bag. Secure it with tape. Have at hand a small sheet of waxed paper and an angled metal spatula.

2. Slide the angled metal spatula under a gardenia to lift and transfer it to the glazed cake, positioning it in the upper half, slightly off center. Surround it with another gardenia, 2 or 3 gardenia buds, and the leaves.

3. Warm the glaze over a pan of hot water until it reaches 90° to 95°F, just enough to soften it. Remove from heat, dry the bottom of the bowl, and spoon or pour the glaze into the parchment bag. Cut a ⅛-inch opening in the tip. Pipe a few test lines on the waxed paper to see if they hold their shape. If the lines flatten, cool the bag briefly. Pipe a simple scroll design on the waxed paper to test it again, adjusting the opening in the tip if necessary. Slip the tip of the bag under a gardenia petal along one side. Pipe a double scroll design following the contour of the cake. Repeat on the other side. Pipe a name in the center of the cake or leave it plain.

Makes one 9-inch, single-layer round cake; serves 12

Enchanted Forest Cake

Here is a fairy-tale cake awash in the colors of autumn and the nutty textures of the forest. To make multicolored chocolate leaves, apply the darkest color first, very thinly, so that the lighter colors can show through it (see page 102). Make as many leaves as you can before the chocolate hardens. They will keep beautifully for several months in an airtight container at room temperature.

24 fresh lemon (salal) leaves

All-American Chocolate Layer Cake
(page 135)

Coconut-Pecan Frosting (page 139)

8 ounces white chocolate, coarsely chopped,
plus one 2-ounce chunk white chocolate
(for tempering)

2 ounces semisweet chocolate, coarsely
chopped, plus one ½-ounce chunk
semisweet chocolate (for tempering)

Yellow, orange, red, and green oil-based
food coloring gel or powder (see page 13)

Several dry Chocolate Spaghetti Twigs
(page 89), optional

12 to 15 hazelnuts and almonds in the shell

1. Wash and air-dry 24 fresh lemon (salal) leaves (see page 68) on paper towels at least 1 hour ahead.

2. Cut the cake into 3 layers (see page 107). Place the bottom cake layer on a slightly smaller corrugated cake circle and spread it with 1 cup of the frosting. Place the second layer on top and spread with another cup of frosting. Spread the rest of the frosting over the top and sides of the cake (see page 108).

3. Clear a 3-foot-wide area of work space and line it with waxed paper. Line 2 large rimless baking sheets with waxed paper, securing it with tape. Have at hand a small pair of scissors, an angled metal spatula, and a latex glove.

4. Fold some of the leaves in half along the center vein. Cut out petals in the shape of fall leaves, in different sizes. The cuts you make on one half of the leaf will be mirrored by the other half. Spread the leaves on the waxed paper, face down.

5. Melt and temper the chopped white and semisweet chocolates (see page 22). Place the bowl of white chocolate in a pan or a slightly larger bowl of warm (88°F) water, replenishing the warm water as needed. Stir it occasionally, scraping the sides of the bowl.

6. Meanwhile, using a gloved finger, lightly touch the surface of the semisweet chocolate, dabbing the excess on the waxed paper–lined work surface. Smear a little chocolate on the underside of each leaf as thinly and unevenly as possible, leaving parts of the leaf bare. Repeat until all of the leaves are smeared. Let set on the waxed paper–lined work surface.

7. Remove from warm water and dry the bottom of the bowl of white chocolate. Pour all the white chocolate in a puddle in the center of one of the waxed paper–lined baking sheets. Using food colorings and the angled spatula, tint one fourth of the puddle yellow, another fourth orange, another fourth red, and another fourth green, cleaning the spatula between each color change. It's okay (and even desirable) if the colors touch and run together. The pool of chocolate will remain fluid longer if you work in a warm room. The faster you work, the more leaves you will be able to make before the chocolate thickens.

See photo, page 106.

8. Lay the underside of the leaf against the surface of one of the tinted areas of chocolate, pressing gently to coat it, but not so hard as to submerge it. Holding it by the stem, drag it across the chocolate surface. Lift it out of the chocolate and rap it several times, chocolate-side-up, on the waxed paper–lined work surface to eliminate the excess chocolate. Examine the vein to be sure it is thickly coated. If it isn't, dab it with more chocolate. Clean the edges of the leaf with your fingertips and place it, chocolate-side-up, on the other lined baking sheet. Repeat to dip the remaining leaves, alternating the colors and dragging some leaves through more than one color. Refrigerate until the chocolate sets completely, about 10 minutes.

9. Beginning at the stem, gently pull the fresh leaf away from the chocolate leaf. If the point breaks, wait until the chocolate leaf returns to room temperature, then reshape it with a pair of small, pointed scissors.

10. Arrange the chocolate leaves on top of the cake, with some cascading down the side, if you like, and others scattered around the base. Tuck a few chocolate spaghetti twigs (optional) in the arrangement here and there, along with some hazelnuts and almonds.

> Makes one 9-inch, 3-layer cake; serves 10 to 12

Chocolate Notes

Use the spatula method to coat the leaves (see page 68), if you prefer. I find it easier to use the dipping method with small multi-petaled leaves.

The leftover chocolate may be eaten, but it is not suitable for future melting purposes since it is likely to contain moisture from the fresh leaves.

❧ Tinting the puddle of white chocolate.

❧ Dragging the leaf across the chocolate surface.

❧ Pulling the fresh leaf away from the chocolate leaf.

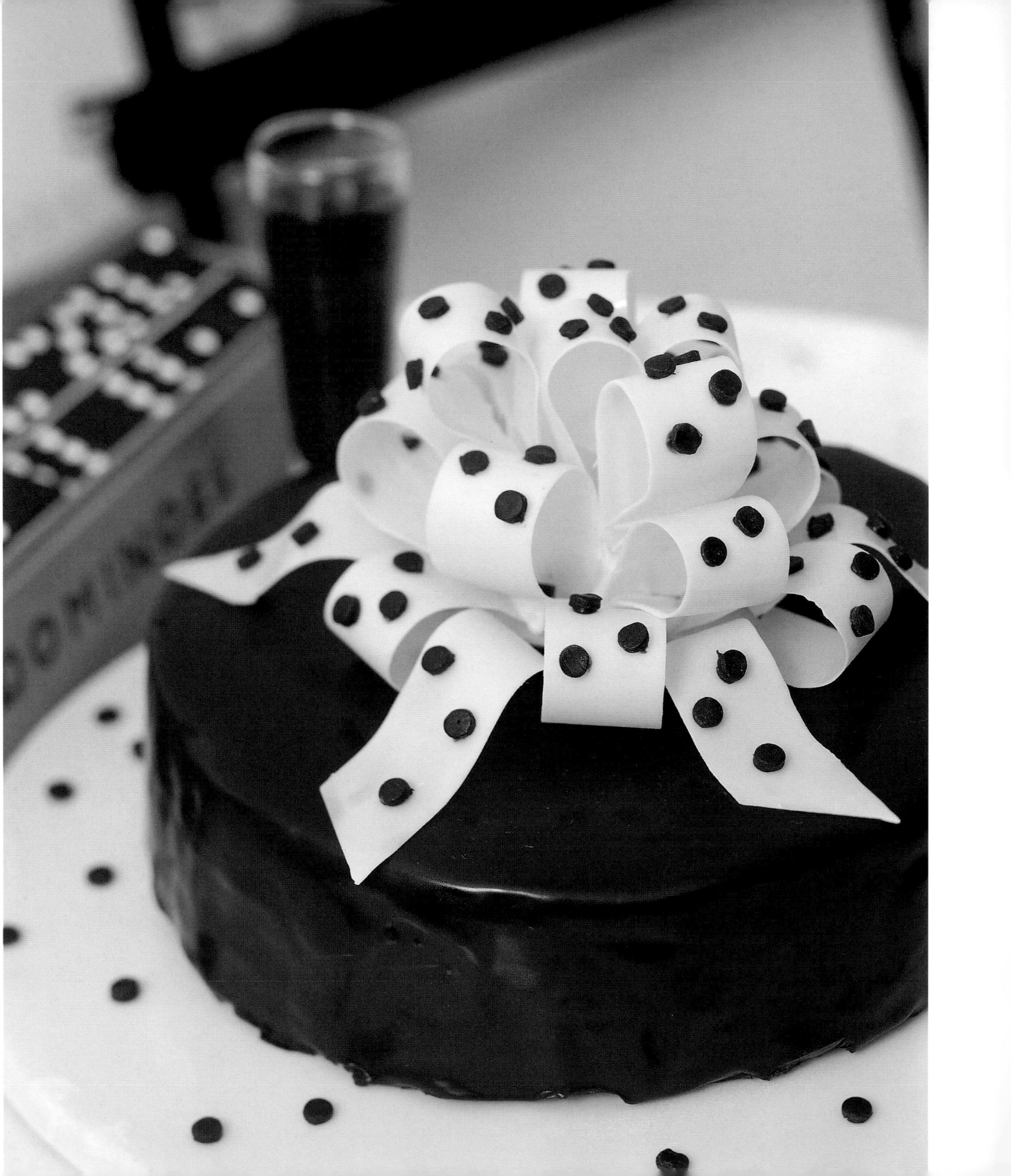

Gâteau Domino

The crisp contrast of dark and white chocolate adds a dramatic accent to this elegant ganache-glazed torte. The polka-dotted bow, which is surprisingly easy to make, illustrates the molding versatility of freezer paper. The matching plate, though optional, makes a knockout presentation for special occasions. The bow and plate can both be made ahead.

Brown Velvet Glaze (page 144)

Chocolate Date-Nut Cake (page 130)

1 ounce (1 ½-inch diameter ball)
  Dark Chocolate Clay (page 77)

2 ounces white or semisweet chocolate, coarsely chopped, plus one ½-ounce chunk white or semisweet chocolate (for tempering)

One white chocolate bow
  with extra ribbons (see page 71)

One 10-inch round white chocolate plate
  (see page 59), optional

1. Prepare the glaze. Use it to "crumb coat" and glaze the cake (see page 109). Let the glaze set for at least 30 minutes before decorating the cake.

2. Clear a 3-foot-wide area of work surface. Have at hand a waxed paper–lined pattern board, an angled metal spatula, a small rolling pin, and a No. 10 decorating tip with a round opening. Cut a parchment triangle in half and roll one piece into a decorating bag, securing it with tape.

3. Using the heel of your hand, knead the clay on the smooth work surface until it is the consistency of Play-Doh: soft and malleable, but not sticky. Place it on the pattern board, flattening it with a rolling pin into a thin strip. Lift it on and off the paper to keep it from sticking. Using the small opening of the decorating tip, cut out about 60 small circles of clay.

4. Melt and temper the chopped chocolate (see page 22). Spoon it into the parchment bag, cutting a ⅛-inch opening in the tip.

5. Carefully attach 2 or 3 dots to each of the loops of the assembled white chocolate bow and the extra ribbons, securing them with piped dots of chocolate. Using an angled spatula, lift and place the bow in the center of the cake. Tuck a few ribbons under the loops, trimming the length if necessary.

6. Slide a long spatula under the cake and place it on a serving plate or on the chocolate plate, if using, securing it with a small piped dollop of chocolate. Attach more chocolate clay circles to the exposed areas of the chocolate plate with piped dots of chocolate.

7. Let the parchment bag sit until the chocolate hardens inside. Discard the paper and store the leftover chocolate in an airtight container at room temperature for future use.

Makes one 8-inch, single-layer round cake; serves 10 to 12

Teardrop Dessert Cups

You'll be amazed to see the ingenious way the chocolate bottoms are attached to these elegant dessert cups. It is truly a case of chocolate sleight of hand! The 8 strips for this project come from very humble beginnings: the 9-by-11-inch clear plastic cover sheets of a report binder, the kind that every drugstore and office supply store sells. To make any occasion special, fill and embellish the cups with cocoa-dusted chocolate mousse and spear them with a gilded filigree chocolate scroll. Serve with raspberry sauce and watch everybody swoon.

With experience, you will be able to make all 8 cups at one time. For now, make 4 at a time so that you don't have to rush to complete the steps before the chocolate sets.

> 2 ½ pounds bittersweet chocolate, coarsely chopped, plus 10 ounces bittersweet chocolate, in chunks (for tempering)
>
> Super Gold Luster Dust (see page 14)
>
> 1 ½ recipes Rich Chocolate Mousse (page 138)
>
> ¼ cup unsweetened cocoa powder (for dusting)
>
> 2 recipes Red Razzberry Sauce (page 142)
>
> About 40 fresh red and black raspberries for garnish

1. Clear a 3-by-2-foot area of work surface and line it with a long sheet of waxed paper. Line 2 large rimless baking sheets with waxed paper, securing it with tape. Line 1 pattern board with paper (see page 15). Fit a 12-inch pastry bag with a No. 1A decorating tip with a ½-inch round opening. Have at hand 3 or 4 parchment decorating bags, a sieve, an angled spatula, a small water color brush, and one 9-by-11-inch clear plastic report binder.

2. Cut the plastic report binder into eight 2-by-10-inch strips. Arrange 4 strips on the work surface in 2 columns spaced about 3 inches apart.

3. Melt and temper the chopped chocolate (see page 22). When not in use, keep the bowl of chocolate in a pan or a slightly larger bowl of warm (90°F) water, replenishing the warm water as needed. Stir the chocolate occasionally, scraping the sides of the bowl. Dry the bottom of the bowl each time you remove it from the water.

4. Spoon some chocolate into a parchment bag, filling it half full. Cut a ¼-inch opening in the tip and pipe a thick line of chocolate across each strip. Using the angled spatula, spread the chocolate in a thin, even layer, extending it beyond the edges. Pull each strip away from the surface, leaving the surplus behind. Clean the edges with your fingertips and let sit for 2 or 3 minutes, or until the surface appears dull.

5. Using the angled spatula, spread 1 cup chocolate in a 6 ½-by-9-inch rectangle on a lined baking sheet. Press the ends of each strip together, chocolate sides touching. Stand the strips, cut-side-down, in the chocolate, pressing gently to embed them. Refrigerate until the plastic strips appear frosted, about 15 minutes.

6. Meanwhile, clear the work surface, lining it with fresh waxed paper. Make 4 more chocolate-coated strips and stand them in another pool of chocolate on the other lined baking sheet. Refrigerate until set, about 15 minutes. Snap off the excess chocolate attached to the molded cups and remove the plastic strips.

7. If necessary, warm the leftover chocolate over hot water or microwave on low (30 percent) power for 10-second increments, never letting the temperature exceed 90°F. Fill a parchment bag half full of chocolate. Cut a ¼-inch opening in the tip.

8. Trace the scroll pattern 10 times on an 8½-by-11-inch sheet of paper (includes 2 extras). Slide the pattern sheet under the waxed paper on the practice board. To pipe the scrolls, touch the pattern with the tip of the bag, elevating it slightly as you move forward and back to the starting point to form the center loop. Repeat to make 2 smaller loops on either side. Beginning at the base of the scrolls, squeeze hard to pipe the spike, gradually lessening pressure as you reach the point. Refrigerate until the chocolate sets, about 5 minutes. Slide the angled spatula under the scrolls and gently turn them over. Pipe over the back of the lines to strengthen them. Refrigerate again, about 5 minutes.

9. To gild the scrolls, lightly touch the surface of the gold luster dust with the watercolor brush, tapping the excess into the lid of its container. Brush it onto the loops, adding more luster dust as needed.

10. Spoon some of the mousse into the pastry bag, filling it half full. Insert the tip deep into the cup, squeezing hard to fill it to the rim with mousse. Level the top with an angled spatula and dust with cocoa. Repeat to fill the other cups.

11. To serve, spear each cup with a gilded scroll and place on a large dessert plate alongside a pool of sauce. Garnish with a few red and black raspberries.

12. Refrigerate the leftover chocolate on waxed paper until set. Store with the surplus chocolate in an airtight container at room temperature for future use.

Makes 8 dessert cups

Chocolate Note
For really gala occasions, these cups may be made with gold-flecked acetate sheets, which transfer gold highlights as well as shine to the chocolate (see page 152).

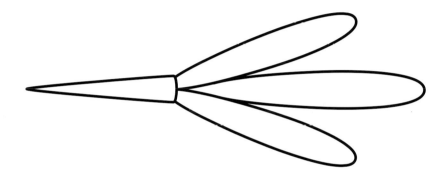

≈ Using 2 sheets of 8½-by-11-inch paper, pipe this scroll pattern 10 times.

Chocolate Fondue Birdbaths with Chocolate Birds

Few of us can resist the urge to plunge fruit, cake, cookies, or fingers into a voluptuous pool of chocolate sauce—especially when it's served in its own edible container. From experience, I know that most guests will beg to take what's left of this novel dessert home with them, so be prepared to supply the necessary "doggie" bags.

8 Chocolate Cups (page 66)

2 recipes Chocolate Sauce (page 143)

8 ounces Dark, Milk,
   or White Chocolate Clay (page 77)

About 80 pieces assorted fruit:
   fresh berries or figs; peeled and sliced
   bananas, kiwis, mangos, or apples;
   candied orange peel or glacé apricots; or
   small clusters of seedless grapes

1. Clear a 3-foot-wide area of work surface. Have at hand a small pair of pointed scissors.

2. You can make the balloon cups up to several months in advance. Make the chocolate sauce at least 2½ hours before serving and let cool to about 82°F to avoid a meltdown when you pour it into the chocolate cups.

3. Make the chocolate birds: Using the heel of your hand, knead a handful of clay at a time on the work surface until it is the consistency of Play-Doh: soft and malleable, but not sticky.

4. Divide the clay into 8 pieces, each weighing about 1 ounce. Roll each piece in the center of your palms to form a 1-inch diameter ball. Place a ball between the edges of your palms and roll it gently to form a 1¼-inch pear shape. Place the narrow end of the pear between both index fingers, about ½ inch from the top. Roll it back and forth to shape the head and neck of the bird. While holding it there with one hand, bend the bottom of the pear upward with your thumb and index finger to begin to form the body. Continue shaping the body by pulling and eliminating excess clay from the tail as you taper and tilt it slightly upward. To form the beak, pinch the side of the head with the tips of your thumb and index finger. Using the tips of the scissors, clip the beak open, then make shallow V-cuts on each side of the body for the wings, and cut shallow feather lines on the wings and tail. Poke 2 holes in the head for the eyes with the points of the scissors. Repeat to make a total of 8 birds.

5. Using the scissors again, cut a small slit on the underside of each bird. Pry the slits open just enough to fasten a bird to the wall of each cup.

6. To serve, place a chocolate cup in the center of a dinner plate. Fill the cup with ⅓ cup sauce and surround it with the fruit for dipping. Pass a pitcher of extra sauce for second helpings.

Makes 8 birdbaths

See photo, page viii.

Chocolate-Almond Pastries

Here is a pretty, make-ahead dessert that actually tastes better after it's been frozen. Once thawed, the crispy layers of dacquoise, which are sandwiched between layers of soft buttercream, become mellow, giving the pastries a wonderful texture that everyone loves. If some of the disks are imperfect or broken, use them in the center of the stack and nobody will ever know.

1 ¾ cups sliced almonds, toasted
  (see page 7)

Chocolate Buttercream (page 140)

36 to 42 Chocolate Dacquoise disks
  (page 136)

Confectioners' sugar, for dusting

1. Clear a 3-foot-wide area of work surface. Cover part of it with a long sheet of waxed paper. Line a large baking sheet with waxed paper. Fit a 12-inch pastry bag with a plastic coupler and a No. 10 decorating tip with a round opening. Reserve ¼ cup of the most perfect almond slices to use for the decoration. Put the rest in a 10-inch pie plate, crushing them gently in your palms to make them adhere better to the frosting.

2. Prepare the buttercream: Using a metal spatula, fill and stack groups of 3 dacquoise disks with about 2 teaspoons of buttercream per layer, leaving the top one bare. Hold the top and bottom of the stack between your thumb and index finger. Using the tip of the spatula, scoop out a portion of buttercream that is equivalent to the height of the stacked pastry. Frost the sides of the disks with it, stroking the spatula side to side to apply an even coat. Try not to get frosting on top. Repeat to frost the remaining pastries, placing them on the lined work surface.

3. Holding the pastries in the same way, gently roll the frosted sides in the crushed almonds, pressing them lightly into place with your hand. Arrange them in rows spaced ½ inch apart on the lined baking sheet.

4. Spoon some of the leftover buttercream into the pastry bag, pushing it down, twisting the bag closed, and grasping it in the crook of your hand between your thumb and index finger. Hold the bag at a 90-degree angle, directly over the center of the pastry, with the tip slightly elevated. Squeeze the bag, keeping the tip submerged in the frosting until a bulb of buttercream forms that is about ⅓ inch in diameter. Stop squeezing and pull away, using the tip to smooth the surface. Plunge the pointed tips of 5 perfect almond slices into the base of the bulb at an angle, forming a daisy. Repeat to decorate the remaining stacks of disks.

5. Store the pastries in the refrigerator for up to 1 week, or freeze in an airtight container for up to 6 months. Let frozen pastries defrost, covered, in the refrigerator overnight. To serve, let the pastries sit at room temperature for 1 hour, then lightly dust with confectioners' sugar.

Makes 12 to 14 pastries

VARIATION:

Bite-Sized Pastries: Use a 1-inch cutter to make the pattern. Fill and ice them with Mocha Buttercream (page 140) and roll them in chopped toasted hazelnuts.

7

basic cakes, fillings, frostings, and sauces

It's easy to get caught up in the fun of making spectacular-looking cakes and desserts and forget that taste is what's really important. The "icing on the cake" in baking, as well as in life, should be just that: the bonus (flavor, moisture, or artistic touch) that enhances what is *already* good. The cakes, fillings, frostings, and sauces in this chapter are the basic components for the spectacular cakes and desserts in this book, and they will guarantee the success of your creations.

Always use quality ingredients—particularly chocolate. While other flavorings merely *perfume* cakes and desserts, chocolate *infuses* them with its presence—which is why the chocolate you use and the way you handle it are so critical to successful baking. If chocolate is the primary ingredient in a recipe, you owe it to yourself to seek out the best-quality chocolate you can find. That may mean splurging a little, but quality begets quality.

Once your pantry is stocked with chocolate, you'll be ready to start baking your way through these pages, learning new techniques and developing a repertoire of recipes to showcase your talents as a skilled chocolate artisan. Here are some do-ahead baking tips to help you get started:

Prepare the baking pans. I dislike greasing and flouring pans, so my recipes often suggest lining the bottoms with a circle of parchment or waxed paper and spraying the sides with a vegetable-oil cooking spray. If necessary, I use soft butter or vegetable shortening followed by a dusting of flour, bread or cookie crumbs, or unsweetened cocoa powder, with the excess tapped out. Pans should not be greased for angel food, sponge, or chiffon-type cakes.

Measure all the ingredients ahead of time. Sift dry ingredients over waxed paper to save cleanup time. Cut butter into 1-inch slices to speed its warming and to make it easier to cream. Weigh, chop, and melt chocolate ahead of time so it has time to cool before you incorporate it into a recipe. Let all the other ingredients warm to room temperature.

Measure all ingredients accurately. Sift flour before measuring it (unless a recipe specifies to the contrary). Sift cocoa powder and granulated sugar if it looks lumpy. Measure liquids in a liquid measuring cup (typically glass or plastic ones with a spout). To do so accurately, place the cup on the counter, fill it, then bend over to read it at eye level. Measure dry ingredients in dry measuring cups (typically metal or plastic nesting cups).

Have at hand all the necessary tools and equipment: metal spatulas to level measuring spoons and cups and to smooth batters in the pan; rubber spatulas for stirring, mixing and folding mixtures; and a 12- to 14-inch-diameter mixing bowl for folding ingredients into one another. The large circumference will enable you to lift and manipulate the batter in the most efficient way, so that no area is neglected.

Adjust the shelves in the oven. Single-layer cakes bake best in the lower third of the oven. Cake pans containing deep batters bake better in the middle of the oven. Preheat the oven before you start measuring the ingredients. Once the baking begins, don't open the oven door until the time is nearly up.

INCORPORATING CHOCOLATE INTO BATTERS

Experience has taught me a lot about incorporating melted chocolate, cocoa powder, and chocolate chips into batters. The following tips are both practical and helpful:

Melted chocolate should be slightly warm to tepid when you add it to batter. If it's too warm, it can melt the butter or cause the eggs to deflate. If it's too cold, it can resolidify in the batter.

Combine creamed chocolate batters with whipped egg whites by folding a small portion of the whites into the chocolate mixture to lighten it, then folding in the remaining whites in 1 or 2 additions.

Combine unsweetened cocoa powder with the other dry ingredients before adding it to creamed batters, usually alternately with the liquid.

Combine unsweetened cocoa powder with the other dry ingredients before folding it into stiffly beaten egg whites.

Before adding it to the batter, dissolve unsweetened cocoa powder in some of the liquid in the recipe whenever possible.

Chill chocolate chips briefly before adding them to heavy cake batters so that they will separate uniformly and not sink to the bottom so readily. Some people flour the chips before adding them to the batter for the same reason. For best results, use mini-size chips in cake batters.

Add chocolate chips to recipes last, so that they remain intact.

White chocolate chips are very heat sensitive and may scorch unless they're totally submerged in batter.

Confectionery coating chips (chocolate-flavored, mint-flavored, natural peanut flavor, butterscotch, and others) are heat resistant enough to cause few baking problems.

MAKING CHOCOLATE SUBSTITUTIONS

Substituting one chocolate for another in recipes can be risky, but sometimes it just can't be helped. Here are some safe guidelines that produce varying degrees of success:

Bittersweet, semisweet, and sweet dark chocolates can be used interchangeably in most baking recipes.

When a recipe calls for melted chocolate chips, substitute an equal amount of bar chocolate.

To substitute unsweetened cocoa powder for unsweetened chocolate: Use 3 tablespoons unsweetened cocoa powder and 1 tablespoon butter or shortening for every 1 square (or ounce) of unsweetened chocolate.

To substitute unsweetened cocoa powder for semisweet chocolate: Use 1 ½ tablespoons unsweetened cocoa powder for every 1 square (or ounce) of semisweet chocolate. Add 1 tablespoon of sugar and 1 ½ teaspoons of butter or shortening.

To substitute semisweet chocolate for unsweetened chocolate: Use 1 ounce semisweet chocolate for every ½ ounce of unsweetened chocolate. Add 1 or 2 tablespoons sugar.

To substitute Nestlé Choco Bake (see page 140) for unsweetened chocolate: Use equal parts.

FREEZING CHOCOLATE CAKES AND DESSERTS

Most chocolate cakes freeze beautifully. Wrap plain chocolate cakes, cookies, bars, and brownies individually in moisture-proof paper such as freezer wrap or plastic wrap. For a really secure covering, rewrap them in heavyweight aluminum foil. Freeze frosted chocolate cakes uncovered until firm, then wrap them the same way in moisture-proof paper. Place fancier frosted cakes in a cake box for protection, then double-wrap the box with freezer wrap, plastic wrap, or foil. Storage times will vary, but most frosted cakes will last about 2 months. Plain cakes, if well wrapped, will last up to 4 months; cookies, bars, and brownies, about 3 months. Do not unwrap frozen baked items until they are completely thawed (preferably overnight in the refrigerator) and brought to room temperature.

Chocolate Cheesecake

I used to be a purist when it came to cheesecakes, always preferring mine plain, with no other contributing flavor. My opinion changed, however, when I sampled this wonderful chocolate version with its crunchy walnut and butter-biscuit crust. Cheesecakes are easy to make, provided the cream cheese is soft before you start to beat it; once lumps form, they will never disappear. For a lighter version of this cake, substitute Neufchâtel cheese (which contains one-third the fat of cream cheese) and nonfat sour cream. Frankly, I think it's every bit as good.

12 ounces semisweet chocolate, coarsely chopped

1 cup (4 ounces) walnuts, finely chopped

1 cup (about 17) Leibniz Butter Biscuits crumbs, finely ground (see Note)

¼ cup firmly packed light brown sugar

4 tablespoons (½ stick) unsalted butter, melted

Three 8-ounce packages cream cheese, at room temperature

1 cup granulated sugar

3 large eggs

1 cup sour cream

1 teaspoon instant espresso coffee powder

2 tablespoons Kahlúa or Tia Maria coffee liqueur

1. Position a rack in the center of the oven. Preheat the oven to 350°F. Line the bottom of a 9-by-3-inch springform pan with aluminum foil, tucking the excess under the bottom plate. Reassemble the pan so that the plate fits securely when the sides of the pan are in place. Lightly butter the bottom and sides of the pan.

2. Melt the chocolate (see page 16). Let cool to room temperature.

3. In a small bowl, combine the walnuts, biscuit crumbs, brown sugar, and melted butter, blending well. Press an even layer of crumbs on the sides of the pan to within ½ inch of the top. Press the remainder on the bottom of the pan, forming a compact layer. Set aside.

4. In a large bowl, using an electric mixer, beat the cream cheese on medium speed just until smooth. Reduce the speed to low and add the sugar in a steady stream. Stop the mixer and scrape the sides and bottom of the bowl. Increase the speed to medium and add the eggs, one at a time, beating just until they are completely blended in. Add the chocolate, mixing just until blended. Stop the machine and scrape the sides and bottom of the bowl.

5. In a small bowl, combine the sour cream, coffee powder, and liqueur. Add the mixture to the batter, blending until smooth.

6. Spread the batter in the prepared pan, leveling it with an angled metal spatula. Place the pan on a sided baking sheet (to catch possible leaks) and bake for about 45 minutes. The center will appear soft, but it will firm up as it cools. Turn off the heat and let the cake cool in the oven with the door ajar for about 1 hour to help prevent the cake from cracking and/or sinking in the center.

7. Place the cake on a wire cake rack to cool completely. Cover with aluminum foil and refrigerate for at least 8 hours (preferably overnight). Release the sides of the cake with a metal spatula. Release the clamp to remove the sides of the pan. Remove the foil-covered bottom plate and replace it with a slightly smaller corrugated cake circle.

Makes one 9-inch, single-layer cake; serves 10 to 12

Chocolate Note
Bahlsen's Leibniz Butter Biscuits, which measure 2 by 2½ inches, are available in the imported-cookie section of most supermarkets.

Chocolate Date-Nut Cake

Dates add an elusive flavor to this rich, moist cake of Mediterranean origin. Most people who sample it, including those who say they don't like dates, invariably ask for second helpings. The cake is especially seductive bathed in a coat of shiny chocolate glaze with a dollop of whipped cream on top. Or, serve it frosted with whipped cream, or dusted with confectioners' sugar, or plain, with a scoop of vanilla ice cream on top.

4 ounces semisweet chocolate, coarsely chopped

1 cup (8 ounces) firmly packed whole pitted dates (see Note)

1 ⅓ cups sugar

½ teaspoon baking soda

½ cup boiling water

1 cup (2 sticks) unsalted butter, at room temperature

2 large eggs

1 teaspoon vanilla extract

1 ½ cups sifted all-purpose flour

⅔ cup sour cream

½ cup (2 ounces) pecans, coarsely chopped

1. Position a rack in the lower third of the oven. Preheat the oven to 350°F. Line the bottom of an 8-by-3-inch round cake pan with a circle of parchment or waxed paper. Lightly coat the sides of the pan with vegetable-oil cooking spray.

2. Melt the chocolate (see page 16). Let cool to room temperature.

3. Cut the dates into coarse pieces and place them in a blender or food processor with 2 tablespoons of the sugar, pulsing them on and off until they are finely chopped. Transfer the dates to a small bowl. Sprinkle them with the baking soda and add the boiling water. Stir until the dates are thoroughly moistened. Let cool completely.

4. In a large bowl, using an electric mixer, cream the butter on medium speed until it lightens in color, about 2 minutes. Reduce the speed to low and add the remaining 1 cup plus 3 tablespoons sugar in a steady stream, stopping the mixer occasionally to scrape the sides and bottom of the bowl. Increase the speed to medium and beat until the mixture is light and fluffy, about 5 minutes. Add the eggs, one at a time, beating until the mixture is smooth and creamy. Reduce the speed to low and add the chocolate, the dates and any unabsorbed liquid, and the vanilla, beating just until blended in. Stop the mixer and scrape down the sides and bottom of the bowl. Add the flour and sour cream alternately, beginning and ending with the flour and beating after each addition. Using a rubber spatula, fold in the chopped nuts.

5. Spread the mixture in the prepared pan, leveling and smoothing it with an angled metal spatula. Bake until a cake tester inserted in the center comes out clean, about 1 hour and 20 minutes. Let the cake cool in the pan for 15 minutes. Release the sides with a metal spatula. Press the edges of the warm cake with your fingertips to make them level with the center. Invert the cake onto a wire cake rack, remove the paper circle, and let cool completely. Place the cool cake, bottom-side-up, on a slightly smaller corrugated cake circle.

Makes one 8-inch, single-layer cake; serves 10 to 12

Chocolate Note
Use pitted whole dates rather than the commercially chopped ones, which tend to produce a drier cake.

Dee's Super-Moist Cake

Cakes baked in a water bath are incredibly moist and seem to melt in your mouth when you eat them. This one is absolutely irresistible. I'm not sure which way I like it best: dressed to kill in a coat of Brown Velvet Glaze (page 144), or hidden demurely beneath a rich layer of vanilla-laced whipped cream. I am grateful to Dee Coutelle, a good friend and chocolate colleague, for sharing this recipe, which I have adapted for home cooks.

¾ cup (1 ½ sticks) unsalted butter

6 ounces semisweet chocolate, coarsely chopped

1 cup sugar

Pinch of salt

6 large eggs, separated

2 to 3 tablespoons whiskey (optional)

¼ cup all-purpose flour

⅛ teaspoon cream of tartar

1. Position a rack in the middle of the oven and remove the top rack. Preheat the oven to 350°F. Line the bottom of an 8-by-3-inch round cake pan with a circle of parchment or waxed paper. Lightly coat the sides of the pan with vegetable-oil cooking spray.

2. In a small saucepan, melt the butter. In the large bowl of an electric mixer, combine the chocolate, sugar, and salt. With the mixer on low speed, add the hot butter in a steady stream, beating until the chocolate is completely melted. Increase the speed to medium and add the egg yolks, one at a time, then the whiskey (optional), beating until the mixture thickens and lightens in color, about 5 minutes. Add the flour, mixing just until blended in.

3. In a large bowl, beat the egg whites and cream of tartar on low speed until frothy. Increase the speed to medium and beat until the whites form stiff, glossy peaks, about 2 minutes.

4. Using a large rubber spatula, gently fold ¼ of the whites into the chocolate batter to lighten it. Fold in the remaining whites in 2 additions.

5. Spread the batter in the cake pan, leveling and smoothing the surface with an angled metal spatula. Place it in a larger but not deeper roasting pan or ovenproof casserole on the oven rack. Carefully add enough near-boiling water to reach about halfway up the sides of the first cake pan. Bake until a cake tester inserted in the center comes out moist but not wet, about 1 hour and 20 minutes.

6. Using a measuring cup with a handle, carefully scoop out some of the hot water to lower the water level before attempting to remove the cake pan. Then, using hot pads, carefully lift the pan out of the water, place it on a wire cake rack, and let cool completely in the pan. When cool, press the top edges of the cake gently to level the surface. Do not worry about the appearance of the crust. Release the sides of the cake with a metal spatula and invert it onto a slightly smaller corrugated cake circle. Remove the paper circle. The bottom of the cake is now the top. It is normal for the surface to be moist.

7. Serve at room temperature. Once refrigerated, this cake loses its soft texture, though its wonderful flavor remains. It can also be frozen. Thaw it wrapped, at room temperature, for several hours before serving.

Makes one 8-inch, single-layer cake; serves 10 to 12

Chocolate-Almond Torte

While vacationing on Spain's Costa del Sol, I couldn't resist exploring Marbella's luxurious pastry shops. That's where I discovered this sophisticated chocolate cake, studded with nuts and infused with the taste of orange, one of chocolate's most complementary flavors. The ground pieces of chocolate added to the batter create a tweedy texture and a wonderful balance of flavors. For a simple but delicious topping, frost this cake with Whipped Cream (page 139) flavored with the grated zest of 1 orange and 1 tablespoon Grand Marnier (or another orange liqueur) instead of the vanilla.

4 ounces bittersweet chocolate, coarsely chopped

1 cup (4 ounces) blanched almonds, toasted and finely ground (see page 7)

⅓ cup sifted all-purpose flour

¼ cup sifted unsweetened cocoa powder

2 teaspoons freshly grated orange zest

½ cup (1 stick) unsalted butter, at room temperature

1 cup sugar

6 large eggs, separated

1 tablespoon Grand Marnier or another orange liqueur

¼ teaspoon almond extract

Pinch of salt

1. Position a rack in the middle of the oven. Preheat the oven to 350°F. Line the bottom of a 9-by-3-inch springform pan with a circle of parchment or waxed paper. Lightly coat the sides of the pan with vegetable-oil cooking spray.

2. Place the chocolate in the bowl of a food processor, pulsing it on and off until the chocolate is finely ground. (If you don't have a processor, chop or grate the chocolate very finely with a French chef's knife or grater.) In a small bowl, whisk together the chocolate, almonds, flour, cocoa, and zest.

3. In a large bowl, using an electric mixer, cream the butter on medium speed until it lightens in color, about 2 minutes. Reduce the speed to low and add ½ cup of the sugar in a steady stream, stopping the mixer to scrape the sides and bottom of the bowl. Increase the speed to medium and beat until the mixture is light and fluffy, about 5 minutes. Add the yolks, one at a time, beating until the mixture is smooth and creamy. Stop the mixer and scrape the sides and bottom of the bowl. Reduce the speed to low and add the ground chocolate mixture, liqueur, and almond extract, beating until just blended.

4. In a large bowl, beat the egg whites and salt on low speed until frothy. Gradually add the remaining ½ cup sugar in a steady stream while beating. Increase the speed to medium high and beat until the whites form stiff, glossy peaks, about 2 minutes.

5. Using a large rubber spatula, gently fold ¼ of the whites into the batter to lighten it. Fold in the remaining whites in 2 additions.

6. Spread the mixture in the cake pan, leveling and smoothing the surface with an angled metal spatula. Bake until a cake tester inserted in the center comes out clean, about 45 minutes.

7. Let the cake cool in the pan for 15 minutes. Release the sides with a metal spatula and invert the cake onto a wire cake rack. Remove the paper and let cool completely. If necessary, trim the sides of the cake with a serrated knife to make them symmetrical. Place the cake on a slightly smaller corrugated cake circle, bottom-side-up.

Makes one 9-inch, single-layer cake; serves 10 to 12

Chocolate Sponge Cake

This cake was inspired by Antoinette Pope's divine French pastry cake, the first cake I ever baked. Antoinette and her husband, François, co-authored several books in the 1950s and 1960s, including The New Antoinette Pope School Cookbook, *which was my bible for many years. The light chocolate cake is wonderful accompanied by strawberries and whipped cream.*

⅔ cup sifted cake flour

⅓ cup sifted unsweetened cocoa powder

1 ¼ cups sugar

7 large eggs, separated

1 teaspoon cream of tartar

Pinch of salt

1 teaspoon vanilla extract

1. Position a rack in the center of the oven. Preheat the oven to 300°F. Have at hand an ungreased 9-by-3-inch springform pan.

2. In a small bowl, whisk together the flour, cocoa, and ¾ cup of the sugar.

3. In a large bowl, using an electric mixer, beat the egg whites, cream of tartar, and salt on low speed until frothy. Gradually add the remaining ½ cup sugar in a steady stream while beating. Increase the speed to medium high and beat until the whites form stiff, glossy peaks, about 2 minutes.

4. In another large bowl, using the same beaters, beat the egg yolks and vanilla at low speed until blended. Increase the speed to high and beat until the yolks are thick and pale in color, about 3 minutes. Pour them over the whipped whites all at once and fold until blended in. Sprinkle the dry ingredients on top, by thirds, folding in each addition before adding more.

5. Gently spoon the batter into the pan. Insert a metal spatula vertically into the batter, circling the pan several times to remove any air pockets. Smooth and level the surface with an angled metal spatula.

6. Bake the cake for 45 minutes. Raise the temperature to 325°F and continue baking until a cake tester inserted in the center of the cake comes out clean, about 15 minutes more.

7. Immediately invert the pan onto a wire cake rack. Let the cake cool completely in the pan. Using a greased metal spatula, release the sides of the cake from the pan. Release the clamp on the outside of the pan and remove it. Slide a large metal spatula under the cake to release it from the bottom of the pan. Place the cake, top-side-up, on a slightly smaller corrugated cake circle.

Makes one 9-inch cake; serves 10 to 12

✣ Gradually folding the egg whites into the batter.

All-American Chocolate Layer Cake

Few cakes are as American as German chocolate cake, which gets its name from Baker's German's Brand Sweet Chocolate, the product that has been synonymous with it since a reader submitted the original recipe to a Dallas newspaper many years ago. I realize that I could be stoned for tampering with a cake so dear to America's heart, but this version, made with brown sugar, has a richer, caramel flavor that I think is worth the risk. Fill and frost with the traditional Coconut-Pecan Frosting (page 139), or fill and frost with Chocolate Buttercream (page 140) and cover the sides with chopped walnuts.

½ cup water

4 ounces Baker's German's Brand
    Sweet Chocolate Bar, coarsely chopped

2 ½ cups sifted cake flour

1 teaspoon baking soda

¼ teaspoon salt

1 cup (2 sticks) unsalted butter, at
    room temperature

2 cups firmly packed light brown sugar

4 large eggs, separated

1 teaspoon vanilla extract

1 cup buttermilk

¼ teaspoon cream of tartar

1. Position 2 racks in the lower and upper thirds of the oven. Preheat to 350°F. Line the bottom of three 9-inch round cake pans with a circle of parchment or waxed paper. Lightly coat the sides of the pans with vegetable-oil cooking spray.

2. In a small saucepan, bring the water to a boil. Remove it from heat and add the chocolate, whisking until smooth. Let cool to room temperature.

3. In a medium bowl, whisk together the flour, baking soda, and salt. Set aside.

4. In a large bowl, using an electric mixer, cream the butter on medium speed until it lightens in color, about 2 minutes. Reduce the speed to low and add the brown sugar gradually, stopping the mixer to scrape the sides and bottom of the bowl. Increase the speed to medium and beat until the mixture is light and fluffy, about 3 minutes. Add the egg yolks, one at a time, beating until completely blended in. Stop the mixer and scrape the sides and bottom of the bowl. With the mixer on low speed, add the chocolate mixture and vanilla, beating until just blended in. Add the flour mixture and buttermilk alternately by thirds, beginning and ending with the flour, mixing each addition just until incorporated.

5. In a large bowl, using an electric mixer, beat the egg whites and cream of tartar on low speed until frothy. Increase the speed to medium high and continue beating until the whites form stiff, glossy peaks, about 2 minutes.

6. Using a large rubber spatula, fold ¼ of the beaten whites into the batter to lighten it. Fold in the remaining whites.

7. Divide the batter between the 3 pans, leveling and smoothing it with an angled metal spatula. Bake until the cakes begin to pull away from the sides of the pans, or until a cake tester inserted in the center comes out clean, about 30 minutes.

8. Let the cakes cool in the pans for 10 minutes. Release the sides of the cakes from the pans with a metal spatula. Invert them onto wire cake racks. Lift off the pans, remove the paper circles, and let cool completely.

Makes one 9-inch, 3-layer cake; serves 10 to 12

Chocolate Dacquoise

Crisp, thin disks of meringue are the foundation for many classic French desserts. When the meringues contain nuts, they are called dacquoise. This dacquoise is especially delectable because it contains unsweetened cocoa, which enhances its flavor even more. The recipe is really quite versatile. By varying the size of your patterns, you can make them small enough to serve as individual pastries or large enough to sandwich between layers of buttercream-filled cakes.

1 tablespoon cornstarch

3 tablespoons sifted unsweetened
  cocoa powder

1 cup sugar

⅓ cup ground blanched almonds

3 large egg whites

⅛ teaspoon cream of tartar

Pinch of salt

1 teaspoon vanilla extract

1. Position 2 racks in the upper and lower thirds of the oven. Preheat the oven to 300°F. Cut 2 sheets of parchment paper to fit 2 large rimless baking sheets. Using a 2-inch round cookie cutter or a compass, trace 40 to 45 circles on the parchment paper, spaced ½ inch apart. Fit a 12-inch pastry bag with a coupler and a No. 10 decorating tip, securing it with a coupler ring (see page 13).

2. In a medium bowl, whisk the cornstarch, cocoa, ⅔ cup of the sugar, and the almonds until well blended.

3. In a large bowl, using an electric mixer, beat the egg whites, cream of tartar, and salt on low speed until frothy. Gradually add the remaining ⅓ cup sugar in a steady stream while beating. Increase the speed to medium high and beat until the whites form stiff, glossy peaks, about 2 minutes.

4. Sprinkle ⅓ of the dry ingredients over the whites, folding them in with a large rubber spatula. Add the remainder in 2 additions, folding each one in gently before adding more. Fold in the vanilla.

5. Immediately spoon half the mixture into the pastry bag, pushing it down, twisting the bag closed, and grasping it in the crook of your hand between your thumb and index finger. Pipe dots of meringue in the corners of the baking sheets to secure the parchment paper, penciled-side-down.

6. Hold the bag perpendicular to the center of the first circle pattern, elevated about ½ inch above the surface. For good control, keep your elbows close to your body, guiding the bag with the index finger of your free hand, which should be positioned alongside the ring of the coupler. Using firm, steady pressure, pipe one long string of meringue in a continuously widening spiral until it reaches the outer edge of the pattern. To stop the flow of meringue, release pressure on the bag, lift the tip slightly, and pull it away. Repeat piping disks until all the meringue is used.

7. Bake the disks until they release easily from the parchment and appear uniformly crisp, about 20 to 25 minutes. Place on a wire cake rack and let cool completely. Store at room temperature in an airtight container. If the disks soften and/or become sticky before using, place them on baking sheets in a 200°F oven for 10 to 15 minutes to crisp them.

Makes about forty 2-inch disks

❧ Holding the pastry bag perpendicular to the center of the first circle pattern.

❧ Guiding the bag with the index finger as the meringue is piped in a widening spiral.

❧ Releasing pressure on the bag and pulling away the tip.

Chocolate Note

To make larger disks for constructing multitextured cakes, trace around cake pans on parchment paper to make the appropriate-sized pattern. Use a No. 12 decorating tip for piping the spirals and increase the baking time to 30 to 35 minutes.

Rich Chocolate Mousse

Because of recent concerns regarding salmonella poisoning from raw eggs, I no longer use them in chocolate mousse. This rich mousse contains nothing but cream, melted chocolate, and a little flavoring. Adding controlled amounts of water to melted chocolate makes it easier to blend into cold whipped cream without having it turn chunky (see page 19). Since all chocolates vary so much, though, be prepared to add an extra tablespoon of water if the chocolate you're using shows any signs of seizing.

6 ounces semisweet or bittersweet chocolate, coarsely chopped

¼ cup tepid water (see Note)

2 cups cold heavy (whipping) cream

2 teaspoons vanilla extract

1. Melt the chocolate (see page 16). Remove the chocolate from the heat source (drying the bottom of the bowl, if using) and add the water all at once, whisking until smooth.

2. Strain the chocolate into another bowl. Let cool, stirring occasionally, until the temperature reaches 90°F, about 10 minutes.

3. In a cold 6-cup bowl, using an electric mixer, begin beating the cream and vanilla at low speed. As it begins to thicken, increase the speed to medium high and continue beating until the marks of the beaters show in the cream. Add the cool melted chocolate to the whipped cream all at once. Reduce the speed to medium and continue whipping just until soft peaks form.

4. Finish whisking by hand until the cream is thick enough to hold its shape. Use at once, or refrigerate briefly if the cream is still not firm enough to use.

Makes about 3 cups

VARIATION:

Flavored Chocolate Mousse: Substitute 1 tablespoon Chambord, framboise, or other liqueur for 1 tablespoon of the water, adding the combined liquid to the melted chocolate all at once.

Whipped Cream

Heavy cream will whip faster and better if everything it touches is absolutely frigid, so be sure to chill the bowl and beaters before you begin, especially if you're working in a warm room. When the cream appears to be thickening, finish whipping it with a whisk so that you can control its thickness more carefully.

1 ½ cups heavy (whipping) cream

1 tablespoon vanilla extract

3 tablespoons confectioners' sugar, sifted

1. In a cold large bowl, using an electric mixer, begin beating the cream and vanilla on low speed. As it begins to thicken, increase the speed to medium high and beat just until soft peaks form. Reduce the speed to medium and add the sugar gradually while beating until the cream falls in soft mounds when the beaters are lifted from the bowl.

2. Finish whisking by hand until the cream is thick enough to hold its shape. Use at once.

> Makes about 3 cups

VARIATION:

Cocoa Whipped Cream: In a 6-cup bowl, combine the cream and ⅓ cup unsweetened cocoa powder, whisking to blend. Refrigerate for 20 minutes before beating. Proceed as directed in the above recipe.

Coconut-Pecan Frosting

No German chocolate cake is complete without coconut-pecan frosting, one of the few nonchocolate recipes in this collection. See also All-American Chocolate Layer Cake (page 135), my variation of German chocolate cake.

¾ cup (1 ½ sticks) unsalted butter, cut into 1-inch chunks

1 ½ cups heavy (whipping) cream

1 cup firmly packed light brown sugar

4 large egg yolks, slightly beaten

2 ½ cups sweetened flaked coconut

2 ½ cups (10 ounces) pecans, coarsely chopped

2 teaspoons vanilla extract

1. In a large saucepan, combine the butter, cream, sugar, and egg yolks. Cook over medium heat, stirring constantly, until the mixture thickens slightly and coats the back of a spoon.

2. Remove from heat and stir in the coconut, pecans, and vanilla. Cool, stirring occasionally, until the frosting is thick enough to spread, about 45 minutes. Use at once, or store in an airtight container in the refrigerator for 3 or 4 days or in the freezer for up to 3 months.

> Makes about 5 cups, enough to fill and frost one
> 9-inch, 3-layer cake

Chocolate Buttercream

Finally! A smooth and creamy frosting that is not overly sweet! You can double, triple, or even quadruple this recipe very easily, provided you have a heavy-duty electric mixer. If you don't, simply make several individual recipes. To make a firmer buttercream for decorating cakes and pastries with fancy decorating tips, use ¾ cup butter and ¼ cup vegetable shortening.

2 ounces semisweet chocolate, coarsely chopped, or two 1-ounce envelopes Nestlé Choco Bake (see Note)

1 cup milk

3 tablespoons cornstarch

1 cup (2 sticks) unsalted butter, at room temperature

1 cup confectioners' sugar, sifted

1 tablespoon vanilla extract

1. Melt the chocolate (see page 16), if using. Let cool completely. (Choco Bake is ready to use.)

2. In a heavy, medium saucepan, whisk the milk and cornstarch together until smooth. Bring the mixture to a simmer over medium heat and cook, stirring constantly, until it resembles a thick pudding. Remove from heat and press the mixture through a strainer into a large bowl.

3. Using an electric mixer, beat the milk mixture on medium speed until the bottom of the bowl feels barely warm, about 5 minutes. (Larger amounts of frosting will take longer to cool.)

4. In another large bowl, using the same beaters, cream the butter on medium high speed until smooth, about 1 minute. Reduce the speed to low and add the sugar gradually, mixing well after each addition until blended in. Add the cool milk mixture 1 large spoonful at a time, beating after each addition. Add the vanilla and the chocolate, beating just until blended.

Melted chocolate must be at room temperature when you blend it into cool frosting. If it's too warm, it will melt the butter and the frosting will be too soft to handle. If it's too cold, it will resolidify on contact, studding the frosting with specks of chocolate.

5. Use at once, or cover and refrigerate for up to 1 week or freeze for up to 2 months. To restore cold buttercream to its original creamy texture, let it come to room temperature before beating it again or it may curdle. If it curdles, briefly place the bowl of frosting in a larger bowl of hot water just long enough to warm the outside of the bowl, which will also warm the buttercream. Beat the mixture again.

Makes about 2 ½ cups, enough to fill and frost an 8- or 9-inch, 2-layer cake

VARIATION:

Mocha Buttercream: Add 1 teaspoon coffee extract or 1 tablespoon espresso coffee granules dissolved in 1 tablespoon hot water along with the other flavorings.

Chocolate Note
To achieve a deep chocolate color in buttercream frostings, I often use Nestlé Choco Bake instead of real chocolate. Choco Bake is a semifluid, unsweetened chocolate-flavored product (it is not real chocolate) that will deepen the color of frosting without curdling or sweetening it. Because it is homogenized, it blends easily without speckling or streaking.

Chocolate Pastry Cream

Pastry creams make wonderful fillings for cake and pastries, adding moisture, flavor, and an appealing texture that is cool and creamy at the same time. This one has the added advantage of being made with nonfat milk, but nobody would ever suspect it.

1 cup nonfat milk

2 large egg yolks

¼ cup sugar

1 tablespoon all-purpose flour

1 tablespoon cornstarch

1 tablespoon unsalted butter

1 ounce bittersweet chocolate, coarsely chopped

1 teaspoon vanilla extract

1. In a medium bowl, whisk together the milk and the egg yolks. Add the sugar, flour, and cornstarch and continue whisking until the flour and cornstarch are dissolved. Pour through a strainer into a heavy, medium saucepan.

2. Cook over medium heat, stirring constantly, until the mixture thickens. Continue cooking and stirring for 1 minute. Remove the pan from the heat and add the butter and chocolate, stirring until melted and well blended. Stir in the vanilla.

3. Let cool to room temperature, stirring occasionally. (This will take about 45 minutes.) Use at once, or press a piece of plastic wrap directly onto the surface to prevent a skin from forming and refrigerate for up to 3 days.

Makes 1½ cups, enough to fill one 9-inch, 3-layer or one 10-inch, 2-layer cake

VARIATION:

Liqueur-Flavored Pastry Cream: Add 1 tablespoon dark rum, Kahlúa, Cointreau, or other liqueur to the warm cream, blending well.

Flavored Simple Syrup

This syrup adds moisture, sweetness, and extra flavor when brushed onto dry cakes.

½ cup water

¼ cup sugar

2 teaspoons liqueur, or 1 teaspoon
   flavoring extract

1. In a small saucepan, combine the water and sugar, stirring until blended. Bring to a slow simmer over medium heat, stirring occasionally. Using a pastry brush dipped in warm water, wash down the sides of the pan. Cover the pan and continue cooking, without stirring, for 2 minutes.

2. Remove from heat, uncover, and let cool to room temperature. Stir in the liqueur or extract. Use now, or cover and refrigerate for up to 3 weeks.

Makes about ½ cup

Red Razzberry Sauce

Raspberry sauce makes an excellent accompaniment to chocolate desserts. Its ruby red color and sweet-tart flavor add balance and contrast to the delicacy of white chocolate and the stronger flavors of dark chocolate. Since fresh or frozen raspberries work equally well, I always save fresh ones for other uses.

Two 10- to 12-ounce packages frozen
   raspberries in syrup, thawed

¼ cup seedless raspberry jam

2 tablespoons sugar

2 tablespoons Chambord or framboise
   liqueur (optional)

1. Drain the raspberries, reserving the juice.

2. In a blender or food processor, puree the raspberries until smooth. Using the back of a large spoon, press the puree through a strainer, discarding the seeds. Scrape the puree from the bottom of the strainer and add it to the bowl.

3. In a small saucepan over medium heat, cook the jam, 2 tablespoons of the reserved juice, and the sugar, stirring frequently, until the mixture boils. Reduce heat and simmer gently for about 1 minute. Remove from heat. Add the raspberry puree and the liqueur (optional), mixing well. Cover and let cool to room temperature. Use now, or refrigerate in an airtight container for up to 3 days, or freeze for up to 6 months.

Makes 2 to 2½ cups

Chocolate Sauce

Most chocolate sauces remain fluid only when they are warm, becoming much thicker as they cool. It took me a long time to develop a fluid sauce that I could pour into my Chocolate Birdbath (page 124) without causing a meltdown. This sauce is delicious at any temperature, so when it's not destined for the birdbath, you can serve it hot, over ice cream, or warm, alongside a plated dessert.

½ cup (1 stick) unsalted butter

½ cup granulated sugar

½ cup firmly packed light brown sugar

¼ cup unsweetened cocoa powder

1 teaspoon instant espresso coffee powder

Pinch of salt

1 ¼ cups heavy (whipping) cream

3 tablespoons Chambord or framboise liqueur, or 1 tablespoon vanilla extract

1. In a large, heavy saucepan, melt the butter over medium heat. Add the sugars, cocoa, coffee powder, and salt, stirring with a wooden spoon until the sugars dissolve and the mixture is smooth and well blended.

2. Add the cream slowly, stirring constantly. Cook over medium heat until the sauce begins to simmer. Continue cooking and stirring until thick enough to coat the back of the spoon, about 8 to 10 minutes.

3. Pour the sauce into a small bowl. Add the liqueur or vanilla, stirring until completely blended. To pour into a chocolate cup, let cool to 85° to 88°F. Otherwise, serve as desired.

Makes about 2¼ cups

Brown Velvet Glaze

This glaze is too good to use only for glazing cakes and pastries. It also makes a great hot fudge sauce that you'll be tempted to eat with a spoon.

6 ounces bittersweet or semisweet chocolate, coarsely chopped

½ cup heavy (whipping) cream

4 tablespoons (½ stick) unsalted butter at room temperature

1. In a food processor, process the chocolate by pulsing the machine on and off until the chocolate pieces are the size of small granules. If you don't have a food processor, use a heavy French chef's knife to chop the chocolate very finely.

2. In a small, heavy saucepan, heat the cream over low heat until bubbles form around the edges of the pan. Pour the cream into a large bowl and let cool for about 1 minute. Add the chopped chocolate granules all at once, shaking the bowl gently to submerge the chocolate in the cream. When the pieces are soft, begin stirring with a rubber spatula until the mixture is well blended and the chocolate is completely melted. If any pieces remain unmelted, briefly place the bowl in a slightly larger bowl of hot water, stirring gently until they melt completely. Remove the bowl from the water and wipe the bottom. Add the butter, 1 small chunk at a time, stirring after each addition until the butter is melted and completely blended in. Strain into a small bowl.

3. To "crumb coat" cakes, let the glaze cool at room temperature until it becomes fudgy, about 1 hour. Use at once, or cover and refrigerate for up to 2 weeks, or freeze for up to 8 months. To rewarm the glaze, place the bowl over a pan of hot but not simmering water, stirring very gently until it reaches 90° to 92°F, the ideal pouring temperature for glaze.

Makes 1 cup, enough to "crumb coat" and glaze an 8- or 9-inch, single-layer cake

Chocolate Note
To maintain its shine, do not refrigerate the glazed cake.

❧ Adding the chopped chocolate granules all at once.

❧ Blending the mixture until the chocolate is melted.

Bibliography

Braker, Flo. *The Simple Art of Perfect Baking*. New York: William Morrow & Company, 1985.

Cakes. The Good Cook/Techniques and Recipes. Alexandria, Va.: Time-Life Books, 1981.

Candy. The Good Cook/Techniques and Recipes. Alexandria, Va.: Time-Life Books, 1981.

The Complete Wilton Book of Candy. Woodridge, Ill.: Wilton Enterprises, 1981.

Heatter, Maida. *Maida Heatter's Book of Great Chocolate Desserts*. New York: Alfred A. Knopf, 1980.

McGee, Harold. *On Food and Cooking: The Science and Lore of the Kitchen*. New York: Charles Scribner's Sons, 1984.

Medrich, Alice. *Cocolat*. New York: Warner Books, 1990.

Pope, Antoinette and François. *Antoinette Pope School New Candy Cookbook*. New York: The Macmillan Company, 1967.

———. *The New Antoinette Pope School Cookbook*. New York: The Macmillan Company, 1961.

Purdy, Susan G. *A Piece of Cake*. New York: Atheneum, 1989.

Walter, Carole. *Great Cakes*. New York: Ballantine Books, 1991.

Welch, Adrienne, and Mary Goodbody. *Unbelievable Microwave Desserts*. New York: Simon & Schuster, 1992.

glossary

Bittersweet Chocolate: Sweetened dark chocolate. Generally less sweet and more intensely chocolate flavored than semisweet chocolate. It usually contains at least 50 percent chocolate liquor.

Bloom: Two types of this undesirable grayish-white blemish occur on the surface of chocolate. Fat bloom indicates the presence of unstable cocoa butter crystals and is caused by improper tempering or fluctuations of temperature. It is harmless and will disappear when the chocolate is melted. Sugar bloom results when chocolate is exposed to moisture; chocolate in this condition feels gritty in the mouth and will no longer melt properly.

Bottom Coat: An initial coating of chocolate or confectionery coating that is applied to the bottom of a candy center to seal it, making the center less likely to leak or crack and easier to dip into chocolate with a fork.

Cacao: The botanical name of the tree, pods, and unfermented beans from which chocolate is derived. The name is derived from the Nahuatl (Aztec) word *cacahuatl.*

Cacao, or Cocoa, Beans: The beans that are found in the pods of the cacao tree. Once processed, they are used to make chocolate. The beans are often classified as criollo (the most prestigious), forastero, or trinitario (a cross between criollo and forastero).

Chocolate: A product derived from the processed beans of the cacao tree. It must contain chocolate liquor and cocoa butter (with the exception of white chocolate, which contains cocoa butter, milk, and sugar).

Chocolate Clay: A malleable mixture of chocolate and corn syrup (or glucose) that is used to model confectionery decorations. Sometimes called chocolate plastic.

Chocolate Liquor: A dark brown, nonalcoholic, semifluid mass consisting of ground roasted cocoa beans. Unsweetened, bitter, and baking chocolate are all different names for pure chocolate liquor, which is also the primary ingredient in bittersweet, semisweet, dark sweet, and milk chocolate.

Coating: A term used to describe a product that "coats" or "covers." It may apply to chocolate as well as confectionery coating.

Cocoa Butter: The natural fat contained within the cocoa bean.

Cocoa Butter Crystals: The fat crystals in chocolate whose structure determines its final appearance and condition. When chocolate contains stable crystals, it has a glossy surface and a smooth texture. Chocolate containing unstable crystals has a dull, blemished surface and a coarse texture. The tempering process creates the proper conditions for forming stable cocoa butter crystals in a bowl of melted chocolate.

Cocoa Powder: Pulverized, defatted, chocolate liquor. See *Natural Cocoa Powder* and *Dutch-Process Cocoa.*

Conching: A manufacturing process of constantly mixing and heating chocolate to help develop its flavor and texture. Chocolate may be conched for hours or days to achieve the desired smoothness and mellow, full taste.

Confectionery Coating: Also known as confectioner's coating, compound coating, summer coating, pastel coating, and chocolate-flavored coating. This product contains a vegetable oil other than cocoa butter, so it cannot be called chocolate. Since the fat in confectionery coating has a higher melting point than cocoa butter, it can be used when the weather is warm. It is available in several colors and flavors.

Couverture: A cocoa butter–rich "coating" or chocolate "covering" of the highest quality. Couverture chocolate usually has a low viscosity (it is very fluid when melted) and a mellow flavor, and is the preferred chocolate for enrobing centers and molding thin hollow shells.

Dark Sweet Chocolate: The sweetest and mildest of the dark sweetened chocolates. It must contain at least 15 percent chocolate liquor and no more than 12 percent milk solids.

Dragée: A small silver- or gold-colored ball for cake decorating.

Dutch-Process Cocoa: Pulverized, partially defatted chocolate liquor that has been processed with alkali to neutralize its natural acidity, reduce its bitterness, and enhance its flavor. It is darker in color than natural cocoa powder, with a milder chocolate flavor.

Enrobe: To cover, coat, or dip something (such as truffles) in chocolate.

Fermentation: A post-harvest, natural yeasting process that kills the germ of the cocoa beans and changes their composition, enabling them to develop a rich chocolate flavor, color, and aroma.

Gloss: The shine on chocolate that indicates it is in good temper.

Leaks: A seepage of filling caused by tiny cracks or holes in the shells of chocolates. Leaks are caused by dipping cold centers in chocolate or by insufficiently coating centers with chocolate.

Lecithin: A natural emulsifier, usually made from soybean oil, that is often used in the manufacture of chocolate to reduce the viscosity of chocolate (it thins it). It may also be used (very sparingly) to help salvage chocolate that has thickened and/or become lumpy. Available in natural foods stores.

Milk Chocolate: A light-colored chocolate containing at least 3.39 percent butterfat, 12 percent milk solids, and 10 percent chocolate liquor. It is sweeter and less intensely chocolate-flavored than dark chocolate.

Natural Cocoa Powder: Pulverized, partially defatted chocolate liquor that has not been alkalized, or Dutch processed. It is lighter in color than alkalized cocoa and somewhat acidic, with a strong, assertive chocolate flavor.

Nibs: Hulled roasted cocoa beans, which are broken up and ground to form chocolate liquor.

"Seeds": Chunks of tempered chocolate that are added to warm melted chocolate to lower its temperature and to create the proper conditions for forming stable cocoa butter crystals. The seeding process results in tempered chocolate.

Semisweet Chocolate: A sweetened dark chocolate, generally sweeter and less intensely chocolate-flavored than bittersweet chocolate. Must contain at least 35 percent chocolate liquor and not more than 12 percent dairy solids.

Shelf Life: The approximate length of time that chocolate remains in good condition. Shelf life varies depending on temperature, humidity, and other storage conditions. The ideal storage condition for chocolate is between 60 and 70 degrees, with 50 percent or less relative humidity.

"Snap": The crisp breaking sound well-tempered chocolate makes when broken. Poorly tempered chocolate, which is soft and crumbly, may bend when broken.

String: The dripping from a dipper's thumb or loop dipping fork that decorates the tops of chocolates. It sometimes identifies the center's flavor.

Tempering: The process of heating, stirring, and cooling chocolate to a certain range of temperatures in order to promote the formation of stable cocoa butter crystals. Doing so allows the chocolate to dry with a glossy surface and a smooth texture.

Theobroma cacao l.: The botanical name for the cacao tree. Coming from the Greek words *theos* (god) and *broma* (food), it means "food of the gods."

Vanilla: A natural flavoring derived from the fruit (vanilla bean) of a vine belonging to the orchid family. Used to flavor chocolate.

Vanillin: An artificial flavoring that is similar in taste to vanilla. Often used as a vanilla substitute to flavor chocolate and confectionery coating.

Viscosity: The measurement of a liquid's "flowability," or fluidity. The higher the viscosity, the less easily a liquid flows, and the thicker it is. Chocolate that contains a high proportion of cocoa butter (like couverture chocolate), has a low viscosity when melted (it's thinner). Melted chocolate chips are viscous, or thick.

White Chocolate: This substance, which is ivory colored, resembles milk chocolate in composition except that it contains no chocolate liquor. It must contain at least 20 percent cocoa butter, 14 percent milk solids, with a maximum 55 percent sugar. Recent changes in FDA regulations now allow white chocolate products to be labeled "chocolate" in the United States, provided they are cocoa butter–based.

White Cocoa Butter Coating: Another name for white chocolate.

mail-order sources

ALBERT USTER

9211 Gaither Road
Gaithersburg, MD 20877
800-231-8154

Carma chocolate, and professional baking and confectionery supplies, including gold-flecked acetate sheets.

ASSOULINE & TING

314 Brown Street
Philadelphia, PA 19123
800-521-4491

La Française, Valrhona, and Wilbur chocolates; plastic (acetate) strips by the box and sheets (large quantities only).

BERYL'S CAKE DECORATING EQUIPMENT

P.O. Box 1584
North Springfield, VA 22151
703-256-6951 or 800-488-2749
Fax 703-750-3779

An incredible collection of imported British tools, equipment, and gum paste cutters (including scriber tools); Peter's Chocolate and chocolate thermometers.

CHANDRÉ CORPORATION

14 Catherine Street
Poughkeepsie, NY 12601-3122
800-3-CHOCLA
Fax 914-473-8004

Sinsation Chocolate Maker (an ideal tempering machine for home cooks), excellent bulk chocolates by the pound, caramel in 1- and 5-pound loaves, oil flavorings, Australian glacé apricots, dipping forks, and beautiful ballotin candy boxes.

THE CHEF'S CATALOG

3215 Commercial Avenue
Northbrook, IL 60062-1900
800-338-3232

Professional baking equipment for home cooks, pasta machines, and the fabulous Pasta-Ezee Motor attachment that converts manual machines to automatic ones.

COUNTRY KITCHEN SWEETART, INC.

3225 Wells Street
Ft. Wayne, IN 46808
219-482-4835
Fax 219-483-4091

A very extensive line of cake decorating supplies and confectioners' tools, including chocolate molds; Super Gold Luster Dust; my favorite oil-based food coloring gels; Nestlé Bulk Caramel in 1- and 5-pound loaves; gold dragées; Merckens confectionery coating and real chocolate; Nestlé Icecap Caps (confectionery coating); Peter's Chocolate in 1- and 10-pound slabs.

FERN CLIFF HOUSE

P.O. Box 177
Tremont City, OH 45372
937-390-6420

Guittard, Merckens, Van Leer, and Nestlé Icecap Caps confectionery coating; Merckens, Peter's Chocolate, and Van Leer chocolate; Nestlé Bulk Caramel; chocolate molds; candy boxes; chocolate chippers; and 12-inch-long glass laboratory-type chocolate thermometers (the kind I use).

GOURMAIL

126A Pleasant Valley, No. 401
Methuen, MA 01844

Cacao Berry, Callebaut, Valrhona, and Peter's Chocolate.

HILLIARD'S CHOCOLATE SYSTEM

275 East Center Street
West Bridgewater, MA 02379
508-587-3666 and 800-258-1530
Fax 508-587-3735

Little Dipper tempering machine (the one I wouldn't/couldn't live without); the best professional badger-hair chocolate-polishing brushes; chippers; sets of dipping forks.

J. B. PRINCE COMPANY

29 West 38th Street
New York, NY 10018
212-683-3553
Fax 212-683-4488

Professional confectioners' tools, including dipping forks, sets of truffle cutters, and chocolate egg molds.

LA CUISINE—THE COOK'S RESOURCE

323 Cameron Street
Alexandria, VA 22314-3219
800-521-1176

A large selection of Valrhona chocolates and many other top European chocolates; De Zaan, Valrhona, and Cacao Berry Dutch cocoas; Valrhona gianduja; chippers; dipping forks; clear acetate strips by the yard. Will ship worldwide.

MACKENZIES' KANDY KITCHEN

1492 Soquel Avenue
Santa Cruz, CA 95062-2111
408-425-1492
Fax 408-425-3759

The United States source for my favorite professional-grade chocolate molds—JKV molds from Holland.

NEW YORK CAKE AND BAKING DISTRIBUTORS

56 West 22nd Street
New York, NY 10010
800-942-2539 or 216-675-CAKE

The best sets of nested gum paste cutters; 8-by-10-inch gold-flecked acetate sheets in several designs; Super Gold Luster Dust (plus other shades); dipping forks; cake decorating and candy supplies; Callebaut, Van Leer, and Valrhona chocolates.

PARADIGM FOODWORKS, INC.

5775 S.W. Jean Road, No. 106A
Lake Oswego, OR 97035
503-636-4880 and 800-234-0250

Guittard, Lindt, Merckens, and Peter's Chocolate; confectionery coating; Nestlé Bulk Caramel.

PARRISH CAKE DECORATING SUPPLIES

225 West 146th Street
Gardena, CA 90248
310-324-2253

An excellent source for professional-quality cake decorating equipment, candy-making supplies, and books on those subjects.

SWEET CELEBRATIONS
(FORMERLY, MAID OF SCANDINAVIA)

7009 Washington Avenue South
Edina, MN 55439
800-328-6722

Callebaut, Lindt, Merckens, and Peter's Chocolate; Nestlé Icecap Caps (confectionery coating) and Bulk Caramel; Bogdon's Candy Reception Sticks; ACMC Table Top Temperer. An enormous selection of cake decorating and candy-making supplies, including scriber tools, gum paste cutters, nonstick rollers, acetate gold and pink transfer sheets, and cotton gloves.

TOMRIC PLASTICS

136 Broadway
Buffalo, NY 14203
716-854-6050

Excellent professional-grade molds in a wide variety of styles and sizes.

WILLIAMS-SONOMA

Mail Order Department
P.O. Box 7456
San Francisco, CA 94120-7456
800-541-2233

Baking equipment, Australian glacé apricots.

WILTON ENTERPRISES

2240 West 75th Street
Woodridge, IL 60517-0750
800-794-5866

The leader in cake decorating tools and supplies, including the best parchment triangles and corrugated cake boards. Wilton Candy Melts confectionery coating.

WORLD'S FINEST CHOCOLATE, INC.

4801 South Lawndale
Chicago, IL 60632-3062
773-847-4600 and 800-366-2462

Cook's Gold bittersweet, milk, and unsweetened chocolates.

credits

The following trademarked brand names appear in the book:

Ambrosia/The Chocolate Resource Diskin Confectionery Coatings and Merckens Rainbow Coatings are trademarks of ADM Cocoa.

Bogdon's Candy Reception Stick is a trademark of Bogdon Candy Co., Inc.

Dröste Bittersweet, Milk Chocolate, and White Pastilles, Dröste Cocoa, and Dröste Praline are trademarks of Dröste B.V.

Sarotti Extra Semi-Sweet and Sarotti Nougat are trademarks of Fabriqué Par.

Ghirardelli Bittersweet Chocolate, Ghirardelli Classic White Baking Confection, Ghirardelli Milk Baking Chocolate, Ghirardelli Premium Unsweetened Cocoa, Ghirardelli Pure Milk Chocolate, Ghirardelli Semi-Sweet Baking Chocolate, Ghirardelli Semi-Sweet, Milk, and Double Chocolate Chips, Ghirardelli Sweet Dark Baking Chocolate, and Ghirardelli Unsweetened Chocolate are trademarks of Ghirardelli Chocolate Co.

Guittard Pastel Ribbons and A-Peels, Guittard Real Semi-Sweet, and Guittard Real Semi-Sweet and Milk Chips are trademarks of Guittard Chocolate Co.

Leibniz Butter Biscuits is a trademark of Bahlsen.

Hershey's Cocoa, Hershey's Dark-Mildly Sweet Bar, Hershey's European Style "Dutched" Cocoa, Hershey's Milk Chocolate, Hershey's Milk Chocolate Bar, Hershey's Milk, Semi-Sweet, and Raspberry Flavored Semi-Sweet Chocolate Chips, Hershey's Premium Semi-Sweet Baking Bar, Hershey's Premium Unsweetened Baking Chocolate, Hershey's Special Dark Sweet Chocolate, and Cadbury Dairy Milk are trademarks of Hershey Chocolate U.S.A.

Baker's German's Brand Sweet Chocolate Bar, Baker's Premium White Chocolate Baking Squares, Baker's Real Chocolate Chips, Baker's Semi-Sweet Baking Chocolate Squares, and Baker's Unsweetened Baking Chocolate Squares are trademarks of Kraft General Foods, Inc.

Tobler Tradition is a trademark of Kraft Jacobs Suchard.

Chocolat Lindt Excellence, Chocolat Lindt Rod Lindtfils, Chocolat Lindt Swiss Milk, and Lindt Swiss White Tablette Blanche are trademarks of Lindt & Sprüngli (USA) Inc.

Dove Dark Chocolate and Dove Milk Chocolate are trademarks of M & M Mars.

Nestlé Bulk Caramel, Nestlé Choco Bake, Nestlé Icecap Caps, Nestlé Milk Chocolate Giant Bar, Nestlé Natural Peanut-Flavored Icecap Caps, Nestlé Toll House Cocoa, Nestlé Toll House Morsels (Semi-Sweet, Mini, Mint, and Milk), Nestlé Toll House Semi-Sweet Baking Bar, Nestlé Toll House Unsweetened Baking Bar, and Peter's Chocolate's Alpine, Burgundy, Broc, Chocolat d'Or, and Snowcap are trademarks of Nestlé U.S.A.

conversion charts

WEIGHT-TO-VOLUME CONVERSION CHART FOR CHOCOLATE

solid chocolate	melted chocolate
8 ounces	¾ cup
1 pound	1 ½ cups
1 ½ pounds	2 ¼ cups
2 pounds	3 cups
2 ½ pounds	3 ¾ cups
3 pounds	4 ½ cups
3 ½ pounds	5 ¼ cups
4 pounds	6 cups
4 ½ pounds	6 ¾ cups
5 pounds	7 ½ cups

SEEDING CHART FOR TEMPERING CHOCOLATE WITH CHUNKS

melted chocolate (at 100°F) Ounces / Pounds	*chocolate chunks* Ounces / Pounds
8 / ½	2 / ⅛
16 / 1	4 / ¼
24 / 1½	6 / scant ½
32 / 2	8 / ½
40 / 2½	10 / scant ¾
48 / 3	12 / ¾
56 / 3½	14 / scant 1
64 / 4	16 / 1
72 / 4½	18 / 1⅛
80 / 5	20 / 1¼

table of equivalents*

LIQUID AND DRY MEASURES

U.S.	Metric
¼ teaspoon	1.25 milliliters
½ teaspoon	2.5 milliliters
1 teaspoon	5 milliliters
1 tablespoon (3 teaspoons)	15 milliliters
1 fluid ounce (2 tablespoons)	30 milliliters
¼ cup	60 milliliters
⅓ cup	80 milliliters
1 cup	240 milliliters
1 pint (2 cups)	480 milliliters
1 quart (4 cups, 32 ounces)	960 milliliters
1 gallon (4 quarts)	3.84 liters
1 ounce (by weight)	28 grams
1 pound	454 grams
2.2 pounds	1 kilogram

LENGTH MEASURES

U.S.	Metric
⅛ inch	3 millimeters
¼ inch	6 millimeters
½ inch	12 millimeters
1 inch	2.5 centimeters

OVEN TEMPERATURES

Fahrenheit	Celsius	Gas
250	120	½
275	140	1
300	150	2
325	160	3
350	180	4
375	190	5
400	200	6
425	220	7
450	230	8
475	240	9
500	260	10

* The exact equivalents in these tables have been rounded for convenience.

index